DATE DUE

THE IMPORTANCE OF

Oskar Schindler

These and other titles are included in The Importance
Of biography series:

THE IMPORTANCE OF

Oskar Schindler

by
Jack L. Roberts

Lucent Books, P.O. Box 289011, San Diego, CA 92198-9011

Library of Congress Cataloging-in-Publication Data

Roberts, Jack L.
    The importance of Oskar Schindler / by Jack L. Roberts.
        p. cm.
    Includes bibliographical references and index.
    ISBN 1-56006-079-4 (Lib: alk. pap.)
    1. Schindler, Oskar 1908-1974—Juvenile literature.
  2. Holocaust, Jewish (1939-1945)—Juvenile literature.
  3. Holocaust survivors—History—Juvenile literature.
  4. Jews—Persecutions—Poland—Juvenile literature.
  5. Plaszów (Poland : Concentration camp)—Juvenile
  literature.   6. Poland—Ethnic relations—Juvenile literature.
  7. Jews—Persecutions—Czech Republic—Brněnec—Juvenile
  literature.   8. Brněnec (Czech Republic)—Ethnic relations.
  [1. Schindler, Oskar, 1908-1974.   2. Righteous Gentiles in the
  Holocaust.   3. Holocaust, Jewish (1939-1945)—Poland.
  4. World War, 1939-1945—Jews—Rescue.]   I. Title.
  D804.3.R63   1996
  940.53'18'092—dc20   95-11712
  [B]   CIP
                                                             AC

Copyright 1996 by Lucent Books, Inc., P.O. Box 289011,
San Diego, California 92198-9011

Printed in the U.S.A.

Contents

Foreword

THE IMPORTANCE OF biography series deals with individuals who have made a unique contribution to history. The editors of the series have deliberately chosen to cast a wide net and include people from all fields of endeavor. Individuals from politics, music, art, literature, philosophy, science, sports, and religion are all represented. In addition, the editors did not restrict the series to individuals whose accomplishments have helped change the course of history. Of necessity, this criterion would have eliminated many whose contribution was great, though limited. Charles Darwin, for example, was responsible for radically altering the scientific view of the natural history of the world. His achievements continue to impact the study of science today. Others, such as Chief Joseph of the Nez Percé, played a pivotal role in the history of their own people. While Joseph's influence does not extend much beyond the Nez Percé, his nonviolent resistance to white expansion and his continuing role in protecting his tribe and his homeland remain an inspiration to all.

These biographies are more than factual chronicles. Each volume attempts to emphasize an individual's contributions both in his or her own time and for posterity. For example, the voyages of Christopher Columbus opened the way to European colonization of the New World. Unquestionably, his encounter with the New World brought monumental changes to both Europe and the Americas in his day. Today, however, the broader impact of Columbus's voyages is being critically scrutinized. *Christopher Columbus,* as well as every biography in The Importance Of series, includes and evaluates the most recent scholarship available on each subject.

Each author includes a wide variety of primary and secondary source quotations to document and substantiate his or her work. All quotes are footnoted to show readers exactly how and where biographers derive their information, as well as provide stepping stones to further research. These quotations enliven the text by giving readers eyewitness views of the life and times of each individual covered in The Importance Of series.

Finally, each volume is enhanced by photographs, bibliographies, chronologies, and comprehensive indexes. For both the casual reader and the student engaged in research, The Importance Of biographies will be a fascinating adventure into the lives of people who have helped shape humanity's past, present, and will continue to shape its future.

IMPORTANT DATES IN THE LIFE OF OSKAR SCHINDLER

1908

Oskar Schindler is born in the Austro-Hungarian town of Zwittau.

1919

The Nazi Party is founded as the National Socialist German Workers' Party.

1928

Schindler marries Emilie Pelze.

1933

January: Hitler is appointed chancellor of Germany; February: Hitler eliminates civil rights of German Jews; March: First concentration camp opens in Dachau, Germany; April: In Germany Hitler stages a nationwide boycott of Jewish businesses; Jewish government workers are ordered to retire; June: Jews and non-Nazis are banned from the legal profession and civil service in Germany.

1935

Jews may no longer serve in the German army; Nuremberg Laws in Germany include denying Jews citizenship and banning marriage between Jews and non-Jews; Nazi symbol, the swastika, becomes the official German flag.

1938

Schindler joins the Nazi Party; Jewish children may no longer attend German schools.

1939

Hitler invades Poland; Schindler arrives in Kraków, Poland; Polish Jews are ordered to wear armbands with yellow Star of David.

1941

Hans Frank orders Kraków Jews to move into the ghetto.

1942

Nazi officials agree on Final Solution at Wannsee Conference; Schindler travels to Budapest, Hungary, to meet with a Zionist rescue organization.

1943

Kraków ghetto is liquidated; Jews are moved to Plaszow forced-labor camp.

1944

The Plaszow camp is liquidated; Schindler moves his factory to Brinnlitz, Czechoslovakia.

1945

World War II ends.

1949

Schindler moves to Argentina.

1963

Schindler is honored as a Righteous Gentile.

1974

Schindler dies and is buried in Israel.

An Unlikely Savior

The freight train slowly pulled into the small town of Zwittau, or Svitavy, in Czechoslovakia on a cold October morning in 1944. Crammed inside the locked cattle cars were three hundred Jewish women and young girls, all cold and hungry, some sick with scarlet fever or dysentery, many near death. Two days earlier they had left Auschwitz, Poland, the location of one of Adolf Hitler's most notorious death camps, where millions of Jews were sent for extermination.

Finally, as the train arrived at its destination, the SS guards slid open the doors and ordered the women out. They marched silently toward the gates of another detention camp, not knowing for sure where they were or if this was where it would be their turn to be gassed to death and their bodies burned.

Suddenly one of the emaciated women spotted a tall, handsome man, smoking a cigarette, standing amidst the Nazi guards at the gates of the camp. "It's Schindler," she whispered to her friend. "It's Oskar Schindler."

Years later Helen Beck still vividly remembered that cold, gray day in 1944 and

Prisoners peer from a railroad car during their deportation in 1944 to Auschwitz, one of Hitler's brutal death camps.

the sight of Oskar Schindler standing at the gates, offering these survivors words of encouragement and hope at a time when it must have seemed like all hope was lost. "Don't worry," Beck remembered Schindler's saying, as the women filed slowly into this concentration subcamp. "You are now with me."[1] And with those simple words Helen Beck and the other women knew they were saved.

A Questionable Hero

Oskar Schindler was an unlikely savior. He was a heavy drinker and a womanizer; he was an opportunist and a crook; he was a profiteer and an egotist. He was also a member of the National Socialist German Workers' Party—a Nazi. But in the end, to more than eleven hundred Polish Jews none of that mattered. To these survivors Oskar Schindler was simply, yet miraculously, a savior.

According to Emilie Schindler, Oskar's wife of forty-five years, this unlikely hero had accomplished nothing before World War II and did little afterward. Yet in between, what he did was extraordinary. "By building his own concentration camp and at great risk to himself, he was the only German in the history of the war to save more than 1,000 Jews from the death camps."[2]

The extraordinary events in the life of Oskar Schindler began in 1939. In September of that year Adolf Hitler, the heinous, or abominable, dictator of Germany, invaded Poland. Soon after the in-

A Survivor Remembers

In the television documentary "Schindler," produced in 1983 for Thames T.V. in England, Ludmilla Pfefferberg, one of the three hundred Jewish women whom Schindler saved from the gas chambers of Auschwitz, talked about the day in 1944 when she arrived at Schindler's camp in Brinnlitz.

"When we arrived in Brinnlitz, it was very early in the morning and it was cold and it was gray. And of course the cattle train was completely dirty. And besides this we were smeared with paint. They smeared us with paint in case someone tried to escape. They could be easily spotted. So we got off the train and one of my girl friends said, 'Look at the chimneys; they are going to get us.' And I said, 'Margot, we are now coming to Schindler. I'm sure they won't do it.' They marched us to the site of the camp and the gates were open and Schindler was there. He was surrounded by SS. He smiled at us and greeted us and said, 'Finally you are with me. So don't worry.' We were with him and we knew that from that time on we were safe because he would take care of us."

vasion Schindler moved to the city of Cracow, or Kraków, the seat of the new Polish government. There Schindler foresaw enormous business opportunities for an eager, energetic entrepreneur like himself, who also happened to be a card-carrying member of the Nazi Party.

Schindler's good looks and easygoing manner charmed both men and women that fall of 1939, and soon he was accepted among the inner circles of the military and the Nazi Party. As one writer put it in a television documentary about Schindler's life, "He could captivate all with his easy charm."[3]

By the end of 1939 Schindler had acquired a small factory that produced pots and pans called enamelware. Over the next two years, as war raged throughout Europe, Schindler watched his business grow and prosper, largely as a result of government contracts for mess kits and field kits and from the Jewish laborers he hired to work in his factory. At first Schindler paid his Jewish employees for their work. But later the Nazis forced Schindler and other factory owners to pay a certain amount of money directly to the SS—an elite and powerful Nazi Party police unit—for each Jewish worker. As a result Jews became, in essence, slave labor.

Thanks to the Nazi government Schindler also acquired a large, elegant apartment, which had been unjustly confiscated from its Jewish owners by the SS. Although he clearly enjoyed his luxurious new home, he was also troubled by the circumstances of the acquisition. In fact years later many of Schindler's friends claimed that he went looking for the previous owners and gave them enough money to buy their escape out of Poland.

Yet as Schindler began to build his career in this occupied city, the horrific events that later became known as the Holocaust were also beginning to take shape. Almost daily Jews were dragged from their homes and sent to forced-labor camps. Often they were brutally beaten on the streets of Kraków for no reason; many were murdered in cold blood. Each month there were new rules and regulations that stripped Jews of their civil rights, as well as their basic rights as human beings.

From the beginning Schindler was apparently deeply troubled by the daily injustices he observed. He had been brought up in a home where prejudice and intolerance simply did not exist. And even though he was an unscrupulous, or unprincipled, businessman, he was also a man who could empathize deeply with others. As one researcher points out, "He was a wheeler-dealer and a con-artist of sorts, but with a conscience and compassion."[4]

Consequently it is likely that Schindler had strong feelings of ambivalence that fall

Oskar Schindler (third from left) poses at a party with SS officials. His charismatic personality and undeniable charm helped him become accepted into the inner circles of the Nazi Party.

of 1939 and spring of 1940. He knew that as a businessman he was benefiting financially from the war. Yet at the same time he was deeply troubled by the Nazis' policy of hatred and persecution toward the Jews of Kraków. Years later the Reverend Moshe Taube, a survivor of the Holocaust who worked at Schindler's factory, offered his view of Schindler's inner turmoil at that time: "I feel that his drinking and his other vices helped him numb his rage against his own people, whom he saw committing atrocities and decreeing genocide."[5]

From the beginning, unlike most other Nazi Party members, Schindler extended respect and common courtesies to the Jews he met in Kraków. Later, as daily living conditions worsened for the Jews, he made a special effort to offer help and simple kindnesses, such as providing food to Jews who had been thrown out of their homes and businesses. "Those who knew Schindler at that time," says Luitgard N. Wundheiler—a psychotherapist and author of "Oskar Schindler's Moral Development During the Holocaust"—"emphasized that Schindler treated the Jews with the courtesy due any human being and with the special friendliness due human beings in danger."[6]

Hitler: A Charismatic Madman

When Schindler first arrived in Kraków, there were 3,250,000 Jews living in Poland. Within five years nearly 90 percent of these men, women, and children would be dead—murdered for no other reason than the fact that they were Jews.

The anti-Semitism, or irrational hatred of Jews, that eventually caused the unbe-lievable annihilation, or killing, of these Polish Jews was not new. Anti-Semitism had existed in Germany and throughout Europe for centuries. Yet on January 30, 1933, a charismatic, or magnetically appealing, madman became chancellor, or prime minister, of the German empire, called the German Reich. He immediately put into motion the horrendous events that led to the slaughter of millions of people. His name was Adolf Hitler.

A Policy of Persecution

Soon after Hitler came into power, he persuaded the German parliament to give him dictatorial powers. He then instituted a policy of persecution toward all Jews living in Germany and began to enact laws that harshly discriminated against Jews.

At first these laws were designed to rid Jews from all aspects of cultural or professional life in Germany. Thousands of Jews who worked for the government or in the entertainment, legal, or publishing professions were fired from their jobs; at the same time, Jews were banned from cultural events and from going to public parks or swimming pools. By 1939 Jews were prohibited from living in many segregated sections of German cities and prevented from walking on certain city streets.

Yet as unjust as these acts were, they were only the beginning of the horror that lay ahead. Within ten years Hitler would put into place what later became known as the Final Solution, the term used by Nazis for the systematic annihilation of all European Jews. Tragically, the Nazis nearly achieved their goal. Out of an estimated 8.3 million Jews living in

German-occupied Europe after 1939, nearly 6 million were killed.

As many as 8 million other so-called undesirables—homosexuals, gypsies, and handicapped individuals, among others— were also brutally murdered during this time. "But it was the Jews alone," says one historian, "who were marked out to be destroyed in their entirety: every Jewish man, woman and child, so that there would be no future Jewish life in Europe."[7]

This policy of annihilation, said Winston Churchill, prime minister of Great Britain at that time, was "probably the greatest and most horrible crime ever committed in the whole history of the world."[8]

Ordinary Saviors

In the midst of the hideous crimes against humanity that were taking place throughout Poland and all occupied Europe, many people simply stood by and watched or later professed, or claimed, ignorance of the events that were unfolding. Yet there were some people, usually ordinary citizens, who put their own lives at risk and stepped forward to help save the Jews from the savagery waged against them. One of these people was Oskar Schindler.

When Schindler first took over the enamelware factory, known as Deutsche Email Fabrik, or DEF, there were only seven Jewish workers. He continued to employ these workers and eventually hired hundreds more "despite attempts on the part of the German officials in Poland to 'aryanize' all factories and businesses, which would have required dismissal of all Jewish workers."[9]

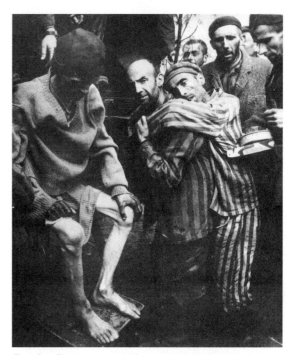

Barely alive, concentration camp survivors are liberated from Nazi Germany. Millions of others, however, were annihilated before the war's end.

Eventually Schindler created a sanctuary for Jews at his factory, where he often hired unqualified Jews who he claimed were skilled laborers essential to the war effort. By 1944 he employed more than one thousand Jews, including some children. "It was employment in Schindler's factory—and Schindler's willingness to buck the Nazi machine to keep them there—that saved the lives of more than 1,100 Polish Jews," explains one reporter.[10]

In the fall of 1944 Schindler heard that all of his Jewish workers were to be relocated to Auschwitz, the infamous concentration camp where on any given day more than nine thousand men, women, and children were exterminated—as many in one month as the entire population of Minneapolis, Minnesota. With expensive bribes of diamonds and other trade goods, Schindler convinced the Nazi officials to let him move his factory, at his own expense, to German-occupied Czechoslovakia, to build his own detention camp there and to take his Jewish workers with him.

The cost was enormous. Not only were there many officials who had to be paid off with diamonds and other valuables in order to accomplish his objective, Schindler also had to build a concentration camp to the government's specifications. He then had to pay a high price for each and every worker he put on his list to go to the new factory.

By the time the war ended, Schindler was nearly penniless, having spent the majority of his wealth in trying to save as many Jewish lives as possible. According to author H. D. Leuner:

> The whole of his considerable fortune was spent on the humanitarian operation, on the bribes he paid to protect the Jews from the Nazi authorities, and on achieving the cooperation of other German factory owners who, at least for a time, fell in with his schemes.[11]

Schindler's Motivation

What motivated this self-centered, fun-loving profiteer to risk his own life to save others? What caused Schindler and a few other men and women like him to step forward when millions of other supposedly good people simply turned their backs on the atrocities that were being carried out every day? These are questions that many people have asked throughout the years since the end of the Holocaust, but few have been able to explain fully. In 1991 photographer Gay Block and author Malka Drucker interviewed 105 people from eleven countries who had risked their own lives to rescue Jews from the Holocaust. They found certain personal characteristics that all of these rescuers had in common. "In addition to possessing an open heart," Block and Drucker re-

A Master Demagogue

Many people wonder how a man as evil as Hitler became so popular. In Never to Forget: The Jews of the Holocaust, *Milton Meltzer offers this explanation.*

"While never letting up on his rabid anti-Semitism, Hitler offered something for everybody except, of course, the Jews. To workers he promised jobs; to employers, fatter profits and freedom from union restraints; to the lower middle class, status and self-respect; to the generals, a glorious army; to Germany, world supremacy; to the nations abroad, peace. He was the master demagogue."

Four years after the war, Schindler (far right) meets in Paris with men and women he rescued from almost certain death.

port in their book *Rescuers: Portraits of Moral Courage in the Holocaust*, "the rescuers, we found, were independent people, some with a streak of rebelliousness and nonconformity, others with an adventurous spirit."[12]

Such a description fits Oskar Schindler, the unlikely hero, perfectly.

The Life of Oskar Schindler

Today much of what is known about Oskar Schindler is the result of extensive research by author Thomas Keneally for his extraordinary book, *Schindler's List*, first published in 1982. Keneally's dramatic account of Schindler's life was based on dozens of first-person interviews with men and women whom Schindler had rescued from almost certain death at the hands of the Nazis, as well as the survivors' own written testimonies now housed at the Holocaust memorial, Yad Vashem, in Jerusalem, Israel. Included among those testimonies is Schindler's own account of the years between 1939, when he first arrived in Kraków, Poland, and 1945, when the war ended.

Psychotherapist and writer Luitgard N. Wundheiler also contributed to the official record of Schindler's life. Among the many interviews she conducted with people who knew Schindler before, during, and after the war was one with his niece, the daughter of Schindler's only sister.

These two important accounts of Schindler's life were added to more recently as the result of Steven Spielberg's stunning, award-winning movie, *Schindler's List*, which premiered in 1993. Soon after the release of the movie, numerous newspaper and magazine articles about or by Jews rescued by Schindler were published, each adding details to Schindler's story.

The Importance of Oskar Schindler

To the eleven hundred Jews who were saved from extermination, the importance

The Consequences of Silence

Pastor Martin Niemoller spoke profoundly of the consequences of silence with these memorable words, as quoted in Scholastic Update *magazine.*

"In Germany they first came for the Communists and I didn't speak up because I wasn't a Communist. Then they came for the Jews and I didn't speak up because I wasn't a Jew. Then they came for the trade unionists, and I didn't speak up because I wasn't a trade unionist. Then they came for the Catholics, and I didn't speak up because I was a Protestant. Then they came for me—and by that time no one was left to speak up."

Schindler stands next to a memorial in Frankfurt, Germany, that commemorates the millions of Jews killed during the Holocaust.

of Oskar Schindler is without question. Without his daring, heroic efforts, they almost certainly would have been murdered, exterminated at the hands of the Nazis.

But there is, perhaps, another reason why the story of Oskar Schindler needs to be told. In the years since the war a great deal has been written about the horrendous acts of Hitler and his followers. But little has been written about those who stepped forward to try to prevent this colossal tragedy, the Holocaust. These stories of rescue also must be told. In the words of Jewish writer Sholem Asch:

> It is of the highest importance not only to record and recount, both for ourselves and for the future, the evidences of human degradation, but side by side with them to set forth the evidence of human exaltation and nobility. Let the epic of heroic deeds of love, as opposed to those of hatred, of rescue as opposed to destruction, bear equal witness to unborn generations.[13]

This, then, is the story of one of those heroic deeds.

1 An Uneventful Youth (1908–1938)

No one could have guessed that one day young Oskar Schindler would be recognized throughout the world as a hero of the Holocaust. Although he was always an outgoing and popular young man, as a youth he showed little promise for greatness and certainly never exhibited any zeal for fighting injustice or protecting the less fortunate.

Yet unlike millions of other people living in Europe during World War II, Oskar Schindler took personal responsibility for the evil he saw around him and did something about it. "If there had been more people like that," says Milton Meltzer in his book *Never to Forget: The Jews of the Holocaust*, "the Holocaust might not have happened."[14]

Oskar Schindler was born on April 18, 1908, in Zwittau, an industrial town that was then part of the Austro-Hungarian empire but at the end of World War I in 1919 became part of a new nation called Czechoslovakia.

His parents were both Germans. His father, Hans, owned a small factory that made farm machinery, which everyone assumed Oskar would one day take over. His mother, Louisa, whom Oskar loved deeply, was a homemaker.

Hans and Louisa had one other child, a daughter named Elfriede. Although she was seven years younger than Oskar, the brother and sister were reportedly very close.

The Schindlers lived comfortably, though not extravagantly. Oskar's mother was a devout Roman Catholic who undoubtedly took her young son with her to Mass until at some later age he rebelled and, like his father, refused to go. "But," says Thomas Keneally, "it cannot have been too bitter a household. From the little that Oskar would say of his childhood, there was no darkness there."[15]

A Popular Youth

In his youth Oskar had many friends, including young Jewish friends. It is unlikely that Schindler ever thought much about the fact that his friends were Jewish. If anything, they were simply friends who practiced a different religion. Schindler "wasn't brought up with an attitude of hate," says Bernard Scheuer, who became friends with Schindler after the war.[16]

In school Oskar was a popular boy, although never a particularly good student. But he loved being the center of attention. It is easy, therefore, to imagine that his boyish pranks often got him in trouble with his teachers, and by the time he was sixteen years old, he was expelled from school for what is reported to be some minor offense.

The Beginning of the Nazi Party

In 1919, when Oskar was only eleven years old, a group of unemployed, right-wing Germans started a new political party. They called their party the National Socialist German Workers' Party, or Nazi Party. (The word *Nazi* comes from the first two syllables of the German word for *national—nazional*.) From the beginning the policies and ideals of the Nazi Party were both anti-Semitic and racist. It was also fascist, a political philosophy that embraces a dictatorial leadership.

As a young boy Schindler probably knew or cared little about the politics of the new party and its anti-Semitic leader, if, indeed, he had even heard about them. Yet the Nazi Party and its politics would eventually have a profound effect on Oskar's later life.

During his teenage years Oskar developed a love for motorcycles. By the time he was in his last year of high school, he owned an expensive motorcycle, which he enjoyed racing.

An Unusual Marriage

In the summer of 1928, at the age of twenty, Schindler met a young woman named Emilie Pelze at a party. Six weeks later they got married. Neither family approved of the marriage. Some say that

Nazi Party members march during a demonstration, carrying flags emblazoned with the party symbol synonymous with hate and intolerance, the swastika.

A 1929 photo shows Schindler and his father, Hans, in Zwittau, Czechoslovakia, Schindler's birthplace.

Schindler may have married her for her dowry, which amounted to a half million reichsmarks. Some reports say, however, that Emilie's father ultimately gave Schindler only a small portion of the dowry.

Oskar and Emilie moved to Moravia, a Czechoslovakian province near Zwittau. Although the couple remained married for more than forty-five years, the marriage was clearly a mistake from the start. Instead of being a faithful husband and family man, Oskar loved to party and have a good time, though not necessarily with Emilie. As Keneally explains, "He neglected Emilie in the evenings, staying late in cafés like a single man, talking to girls neither nunlike nor gracious."[17]

Somehow his young bride learned to accept Schindler's carousing and womanizing. "It didn't bother me at all," she stoically claimed years later. "You can't change a man who's like that."[18] Many years later she would even develop a close friendship with one of her husband's mistresses.

Oskar and Emilie never had any children, although Schindler reportedly fathered twins by another woman during the early 1930s and later, during the war, a third child. Yet he clearly loved children and during the war reportedly helped smuggle young Jewish children out of the ghetto.

Early Career

For the first eleven years of his marriage, Schindler led a rather mundane, or

A Son's Anger

Schindler never forgave his father for divorcing his mother. Yet in many ways Schindler was as guilty of deserting his own wife as Hans was in leaving Louisa, as this excerpt from Thomas Keneally's book Schindler's List *explains.*

"Oskar hated him [for leaving Louisa] and went and drank tea with his aunts and denounced Hans to them and, even in cafes, made speeches about his father's treachery to a good woman. He seems to have been blind to the resemblance between his own faltering marriage and his parents' broken one. . . . When his mother died, he rushed back to Zwittau and stood beside his aunts; his sister, Elfriede; and his wife, Emilie, on one side of the grave, while the treacherous Hans stood solitary—except, of course, for the parish priest—at the head of the coffin. Louisa's death had consecrated the enmity between Oskar and Hans. Oskar couldn't see it—only the women could—that Hans and Oskar were in fact two brothers separated by the accident of paternity."

ordinary, life professionally. After spending time in the Czechoslovakian army, he went to work for his father.

In 1935, when Oskar was twenty-seven years old, his father's business went bankrupt. Soon afterward Hans left Louisa, something Schindler would never forgive his father for doing. According to Wundheiler, "Oskar felt angry and outraged. He sided against his father to the point where he would talk about him in cafes and accuse him of having betrayed a good woman."[19] Not long afterward his mother died.

After his father's business went bankrupt, Schindler took a job as a salesman for an electrical company. In 1938 he joined the local Nazi Party. His party membership had less to do with politics than with good business. He shrewdly realized that as a Nazi he had many more opportunities for doing business with clients who shared the same politics. Says Wundheiler:

> What Schindler knew about the policies of Nazi Germany at that time is uncertain, but it is clear, beyond the shadow of a doubt that Schindler's patriotism had nothing in common with the Nazi racial ideology. Schindler remained free from any kind of racial or national prejudice and continued to count Jews and Czechs among his friends.[20]

By the time Schindler joined the Nazi Party, Adolf Hitler had been dictator of Germany for more than five years. During that time he had issued many anti-Jewish decrees that had stripped German Jews of their basic human rights as citizens.

Schindler must have been aware of these discriminatory laws and perhaps even observed, on his sales trips, the results of these laws. He may even have seen pictures in the newspaper of Jews being marched through the streets of Berlin, carrying signs that read, "I am a Jewish pig."

Hitler's goal at that time was to "reunite all peoples of Germanic language, culture and 'race'" as part of the German Reich.[21] In the spring of 1938 he easily conquered Austria. Later that year he invaded western Czechoslovakia, known as the Sudetenland, where many Germans lived, including the Schindlers. According to Keneally, Schindler was "appalled by the new regime's bullying of the Czech population [and] by the seizure of Czech property"—acts that would soon become commonplace in a world Schindler was about to enter.[22] At that time Hitler

A 1934 anti-Jewish newspaper accuses the Jews of causing the ills of society. Such propaganda fueled Hitler's plan to foment hatred toward Jews.

A Canadian journalist who met Schindler in 1949 found him to be immensely charming, as this description, quoted in Elinor J. Brecher's book Schindler's Legacy, *reveals.*

He was "a man of convincing honesty and outstanding charm. Tall, erect, with broad shoulders and a powerful trunk, he usually has a cheerful smile on his strong face. His frank, gray-blue eyes smile too, except when they tighten in distress as he talks of the past. Then his whole jaw juts out belligerently and his great fists are clutched and pounded in slow anger. When he laughs, it is a boyish and hearty laugh, one that all his listeners enjoy to the full."

promised that the Sudetenland would be his last territorial objective.

Schindler, the German Spy

In the fall of 1938 Schindler met an officer in the Abwehr, the German intelligence corps, who encouraged him to become an agent for the Abwehr to supply military and industrial information about areas of Poland where he had business contacts. Even though Schindler had been disillusioned by Germany's actions in his homeland, he agreed to take on the new assignment for one reason. It meant he would not be drafted into the military service again.

Schindler may have also realized that his role as a spy was one that suited him well. And he was right. As Keneally states, "On his Polish journeys for the Abwehr, he showed a gift for charming news out of people, especially in a social setting—at a

dinner table, over cocktails."[23] It was a skill he would later use to his own advantage—and to the advantage of Jews he saved from extermination.

A Prophet of Doom

In January of the following year, Adolf Hitler spoke to the Reichstag, the German Parliament, inexplicably blaming Jewish businessmen for leading the world toward war, and warning of the consequences of such a war:

> Today, I will once more be a prophet. If the international Jewish financiers in and outside Europe should succeed in plunging the nations once more into a world war, then the result will . . . [be] the annihilation of the Jewish race throughout Europe.[24]

Seven months later, the world was at war.

Chapter

2 The Rise of Adolf Hitler

How could a madman become the political leader of a civilized empire? It is a question that is almost impossible to fathom and is certainly difficult to answer. Yet in 1933 a madman, a lunatic, a callous savage who would eventually be responsible for the deaths of more than six million Jews and millions of other human beings became chancellor of the civilized empire of Germany.

Clearly Hitler's rise to power did not happen overnight. In fact it had begun nearly fourteen years earlier, in a beer hall in Munich, Germany. There on a night in 1919 a thirty-year-old Adolf Hitler first spoke in a frenzy about the need to remove all Jews from the German empire. Breaking into a sweat, his whole body shaking from hatred and anger, Hitler shrieked his venomous propaganda, promising the crowd on that night that he would "struggle until the last Jew is removed from the German empire."[25]

Twenty-five years later he had nearly achieved his most despicable goal.

Adolf Hitler was born in 1889 in a small town in Austria. As a young boy he was a lackadaisical, or lazy, student, "a moody daydreamer who lacked industry and purpose."[26] When he was in his early teens, he dropped out of school.

In 1907, when he was eighteen years old, Hitler tried to enroll in an art school in Vienna but was rejected as not having enough promise. For the next six years he did little to earn a living, subsisting instead on welfare and charity. He earned what meager living he could by working as a manual laborer by day and painting postcards at night. Often he was homeless and was forced to take shelter wherever he could find it.

World War I

When he was twenty-four years old Hitler moved to Munich, Germany. "He wanted to escape military service in the Austrian army," says Milton Meltzer, "because he refused to bear arms with Jews, Czechs, and Slavs."[27] One year later, on July 28, 1914, Austria declared war on Serbia, at that time a small independent kingdom. All of the European countries took sides. Germany and Italy sided with Serbia, while Russia, France, and Great Britain sided with Austria. Within a week all of Europe was engaged in what became World War I.

Adolf Hitler fought in the war until October 1918, when an eye injury forced him to retire. Soon afterward Germany surrendered, signing the Treaty of Versailles.

Unsuccessful as a student or artist, Hitler, far left, joined the German military at age twenty-four. Hitler and others scapegoated the Jews for the country's deplorable economic conditions after Germany's defeat in World War I.

For most Germans it was a humiliating defeat. As part of the treaty, Germany was supposed to pay billions of dollars to Great Britain, France, and Italy as compensation for their losses during the war. Soon, however, Germany was in a state of depression and in the midst of an economic crisis. Paper money was worthless, and millions of people were out of work. So, by 1929, the war debt was cut in half, and by 1932, the debt was canceled.

Hitler was devastated by his adopted country's defeat, and like many other Germans, he looked for someone to blame for the country's economic conditions. The Jews were a likely target. Author H. D. Leuner says: "The Jews were scapegoats for economic crises, unemployment, and corruption scandals."[28]

Following the war, in 1919 Germany formed a new democratic government called the Weimar Republic. It included a president, a prime minister, and a parliament, called the Reichstag. The new constitution also included an article that made it possible for the president to take complete control of the government in an emergency. In other words, it was now possible for the president to declare a state of emergency and become dictator.

That same year Hitler met some of the founding members of the Nazi Party one night in a beer hall in Munich. He soon learned that the party shared his social and political ideals, which were based on racism and anti-Semitism. He became the seventh member of the party.

Hitler was not a particularly intelligent man. Yet within two years he had become the leader of the Nazi Party. Soon everyone throughout the world would know his name.

An Odd and Unlikely Magnetism

In his book Never to Forget: The Jews of the Holocaust, *Milton Meltzer writes about an odd and unlikely magnetism that Hitler was able to exert over people, given his character and demeanor, or behavior.*

"It is hard to understand his effectiveness when one listens today to recordings of his radio speeches. His voice is shrill, hysterical, coarse. His speeches seem only a string of slogans. And his physical appearance was unimpressive, too. Pictures show him as short and flabby, and that little toothbrush mustache is ridiculous. Many who knew him have said that his mind was mediocre. He liked nothing better than to eat sweets and talk about his loyal dogs and his war record. Movie musicals were his favorite entertainment. [Yet] whatever it was, something about Hitler persuaded people to regard him as their messiah [savior]."

Despite his shrill voice and unimpressive physical stature, Hitler had an unusual magnetism that attracted scores of followers.

In 1920 the Nazis published their party's twenty-five-point program, which called for the uniting of all Germans within one greater Germany. Point four of the program was ominously foreboding. "Only nationals can be citizens of the State," it said. "Only persons of German blood can be nationals, regardless of religious affiliation. No Jew can therefore be a German National."[29] Fifteen years later, on November 14, 1935, this point became law.

In 1923 the Nazis attempted to take over Bavaria, a state in southern Germany. They failed, and Hitler was arrested, tried for treason, and sentenced to five years in prison. Eight months later he was released on parole.

Mein Kampf: **A Blueprint for Tragedy**

While in prison, Hitler found time to put his beliefs into a book called *Mein Kampf* [*My Struggle*], in which he referred to the Germans as the master race, "the highest species of humanity on this earth."[30] This so-called master race of white, non-Jewish Germans became known as the Aryan race. For the Nazis, the typical Aryan was blond, blue-eyed, and tall.

The Jews, on the other hand, were considered *Untermenschen*, "subhumans." As Martin Gilbert points out in his book *The Holocaust: A History of the Jews in Europe During the Second World War*: "In Hitler's phraseology [wording] and in the Nazi propaganda, the Jews were an evil disease, poisoning the blood of decent humanity, a conscious plaque-bacillus infecting the pure, innocent 'Aryan'."[31]

In *Mein Kampf* Hitler incorrectly wrote about the Jews as a race of people, rather than members of a religion. "The Jews are undoubtedly a race," he said, "but not human. They cannot be human in the sense of being an image of God, the Eternal. The Jews are an image of the devil. Jewry means the racial tuberculosis of the nation."[32]

Mein Kampf clearly outlined Hitler's beliefs and political philosophy, as well as his insidious, or calculating, plan for Germany and the world. When it was first published, however, most people viewed it as poorly written and unimportant. Some Nazi Party members even referred to it as "that silly

While in prison, Hitler laid out his plans for German world domination in his book Mein Kampf.

book." They were wrong, of course, to dismiss it. As Azriel Eisenberg points out in *Witness to the Holocaust,* "*Mein Kampf* was a blueprint of the actual tragedy as it unfolded later step by step. No one can deny that he gave full warning of what he intended when he came to power."[33]

Anti-Semitism

Know, Christian, that next to the devil thou hast no enemy more cruel, more venomous and violent than a true Jew. Their synagogues should be set on fire, and whatever does not burn up should be covered or spread over with dirt so that no one may ever be able to see a cinder or stone of it.[34]

These words, of course, are shocking. Yet they were not spoken by Adolf Hitler, the most notorious anti-Semite in history. Rather, they are the words written in 1543 by the Christian leader Martin Luther, an Augustinian monk, theologian, Biblical scholar, and professor.

For centuries before Adolf Hitler came to power, hatred of Jews existed. But it was not until 1879, ten years before Hitler was born, that this hatred had a word to describe it. That year a German journalist named Wilhelm Marr coined the word *anti-Semitism* and founded the League of Anti-Semites. The stated goal of the league was "to save the German fatherland from complete Judaization."[35] Marr claimed that the Germans, or Aryans as he called them, were the master race and the Jews, or Semites, were an inferior race.

By the turn of the century a number of anti-Semitic political leaders had been elected to the Reichstag. Yet it was Hitler who was able to capitalize on this long history of anti-Semitism and put into motion the near total destruction of the Jewish people.

The Growth of the Nazi Party

By 1926 the Nazi Party had grown to seventeen hundred members. Among them were two special groups: one, a brown-uniformed group of storm troopers known as brown shirts, whose job it was to defend party meetings from attack; the other, a black-uniformed Schutzstaffel, or SS, which was to provide protection for Hitler and other high-ranking officials of the Nazi Party. (Later the SS also included the Gestapo as well as garrisons that ran the Nazi concentration and death camps.)

Two years later the Nazi Party won 12 seats in the Reichstag in the German national elections. In the 1930 elections that number rose to 107. Suddenly the Nazi Party was no longer an insignificant right-wing group; it was the second-largest party in the state.

During these years Germany experienced serious economic problems, which Hitler and the Nazi Party blamed on the Jews. One Jew living in Germany at the time later talked about hearing Hitler's frightening condemnation of the Jews on radio broadcasts. "He called us parasites," she said. "Hitler would scream and yell, and the radio would shake, or seem to, when he spoke. People were frightened to listen to him. Terror would reach out to us through the radio."[36]

Most people chose to disregard Hitler's outrageous claims. As one writer puts it, "It was especially hard for German Jews to believe that *Mein Kampf* and the Nazi program were more than the projections of a deranged rabble rouser."[37]

Gradually anti-Semitism, bigotry, and intolerance became acceptable behavior as more and more people joined the Nazi Party and supported Hitler's doctrines. In the election for president of Germany in July 1932, the Nazi Party won 230 of the 608 seats in the Reichstag, more than any other party. Hitler came in second in his bid for the presidency, winning almost 36 percent of the vote. Nearly 14 million people had come under the spell of this evil, yet charismatic, demagogue.

As a result, President Paul von Hindenburg offered Hitler the position of vice chancellor. Six months later, on January 30, 1933, President Hindenburg named Hitler chancellor, the most powerful position in the German government. Hitler was forty-three years old.

One People; One Government; One Leader

Hitler came to power in 1933 with a long-standing policy of hatred and intolerance toward Jews. Soon, however, this policy was translated into law, as one by one new decrees were issued, designed to both dehumanize Jews and remove all of their civil rights.

First, Hitler issued a ban on all public meetings that he felt were a threat to public security. That same month, he ordered the establishment of a special prison, or camp, where he would send enemies of the Nazi Party. This camp, which later became known as a concentration camp, was in Dachau, a town near Munich. Later six of these concentration camps, including Dachau, Treblinka, and Auschwitz, became death camps, where millions of Jews were gassed to death.

Hitler accepts the most powerful position in Germany as he is named chancellor in 1933. Seeking to deprive Jews of all their civil rights, Hitler immediately implemented anti-Jewish laws.

Most significantly, in March 1933 Hitler persuaded the parliament to pass the Enabling Act, which gave the new government dictatorial powers. He exercised those powers immediately by announcing the following month a one-week boycott of all Jewish-owned businesses—the first official governmental action against Jews. To help him carry out this boycott, Hitler called on his storm troops, the Sturmabteilung (SA), to picket Jewish-owned stores. The SA painted "Jude" (Jew) on the shop windows and stood in front of the stores, holding signs that read: "Don't buy from Jews!" Although the SA had been ordered not to attack anyone physically, they shouted vicious anti-Semitic epithets, or names, and generally terrorized Jewish citizens.

The same month the Nazis issued the first anti-Jewish law. It said that Jews could not hold jobs in the government, whether those jobs were clerical or professional. That same day another decree was issued that prevented Jews from becoming lawyers. A few weeks later another law drastically limited the number of Jews who could attend colleges or universities.

The Nazis also banned and burned thousands of books, including all those that were written either by or about a Jew. One famous author whose work was destroyed was nineteenth-century German-Jewish poet Heinrich Heine. More than one hundred years earlier, in a premonition, perhaps, of what was to come, Heine wrote, "Those who begin by burning books end by burning people."[38]

SA members confiscate books written by or about Jews, considering them to be threatening to the Nazi cause.

Anti-Semitic literature was published and widely circulated, including some children's books that proclaimed Jews as "shameful, sneaky, ugly scoundrels and Germans as proud, strong, and handsome masters."[39] One book for children that was published in 1936 was titled *Don't Trust a Fox in the Chicken Coop or a Jew at His Word.* This portrayal of Jews as evil and fearsome was instilled in children from an early age. "If you're bad, I'll turn you over to the Jews" was a warning anti-Semitic parents often issued to their children.[40]

In August 1934 President Hindenburg died. Hitler immediately combined the offices of president and chancellor into one, giving himself the title of führer, or leader.

A Blueprint for Tragedy

In his book Witness to the Holocaust, *Azriel Eisenberg talks about how inconceivable Hitler's plan was, even though he had clearly foretold his intentions in* Mein Kampf.

"*Mein Kampf* was a blueprint of the actual tragedy as it unfolded later step by step. No one can deny that [Hitler] gave full warning of what he intended when he came to power. Why, then, did he get away with it? Perhaps because his program [systematic massacre] was so preposterous and grotesque that it was utterly inconceivable. Even when the blueprint began to take on reality, his victims, including the Jews, continued in their delusion that it just could not happen."

The Nuremberg Laws

In September 1935 the Nazi Party held its annual political convention in Nuremberg, Germany. Two of the most devastating anti-Semitic laws were passed. These laws, and thirteen additional decrees that soon followed, became known as the Nuremberg Laws of September 1935. They not only stripped Jews of their citizenship, but also took away all of the privileges and rights that citizens enjoy, including the right to vote and the right to hold public office. In addition, the new laws placed a ban on marriage between Jews and non-Jews and invalidated all such marriages before the date of the decree.

The year 1938 brought about numerous other decrees. Hitler issued a ban on Jews' practicing law, and Jewish doctors were told they were no longer doctors, but merely medical assistants. Jewish children were expelled from schools.

German schoolchildren were taught intolerence against Jews at a young age. A page from a schoolbook depicts an Aryan German as strong and handsome and a Jew as fat and unattractive.

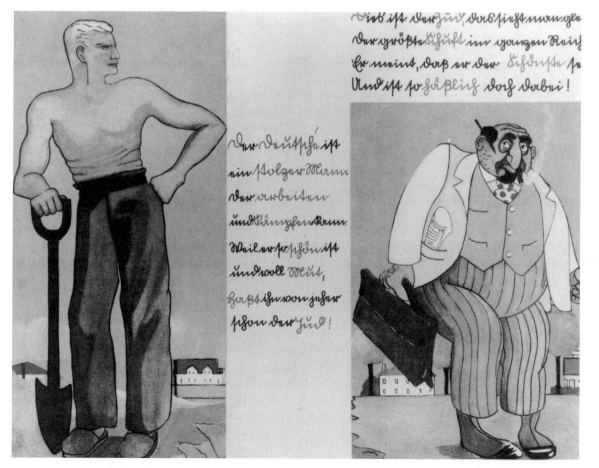

Nazi youth gather around a sign that carries the motto "The Jews are our misfortune." Similar anti-Semitic signs appeared throughout Germany.

In August of that year the Reichstag issued a list of approved given names that Jews could have. Any male whose name was not on the approved list had to adopt and use the name Israel; any female, Sarah. This law made it easier to identify Jews on their official papers and passports. By October of that year all Jewish passports had to be stamped with a J, for Jude.

Kristallnacht

On the night of November 9, 1938, the Nazis mounted a nationwide anti-Semitic riot. Mobs of SA troops raced through the streets terrorizing Jews and destroying Jewish property. Nearly every synagogue in Germany was destroyed, while thousands of Jewish businesses were looted and private homes vandalized. Thousands of Jews were rounded up and sent to concentration camps. At least one hundred Jews were killed. This night became known as Kristallnacht, the "Night of the Broken Glass."

Before Kristallnacht, despite the tumultuous times, many Jews had believed that Nazism would soon end and that things would return to normal. After all, they reasoned, Jews had lived in Germany and had been a part of German society and culture for more than one thousand years. After Kristallnacht, for many the Nazis' long-term objectives became horrifyingly clear.

Chapter

3 Arrival in Kraków (1939–1940)

On September 1, 1939, Hitler invaded Poland in a swift air and ground military maneuver known as a blitzkrieg. Within three weeks, despite fierce fighting Germany's aggressive tanks and well-organized troops defeated the Polish army, which included more than 100,000 Polish Jews.

Most of those Polish Jews were either killed during the fighting or taken prisoner. One soldier who was wounded, but who survived the blitzkrieg, was named Leopold (Poldek) Pfefferberg. Years later Pfefferberg would play an instrumental role in bringing the heroic life of Oskar Schindler to the public's attention.

The invasion was not without its humiliating and tragic consequences for Jewish civilians, as well as the Polish troops. According to historian Martin Gilbert:

> In every conquered town and village, the Germans forced the Jews to clear rubble, to carry heavy loads, to hand over any gold, silver, or jewelry, to scrub floors and lavatories with their prayer shawls, and to dance in front of their captors.[41]

At the same time, thousands of Jews were brutalized and murdered. Often entire families were wiped out.

Two days after the invasion of Poland, Great Britain and France declared war on Germany, which signaled the beginning of World War II. Later they were joined in the war by the USSR and the United States, while Italy sided with Germany. Yet during the first year of the war, Germany's armies seemed unstoppable. In almost rapid

In 1939 Nazi soldiers roll through a demolished Polish town following Hitler's blitzkrieg. This brazen act of aggression against Poland triggered the start of World War II.

succession Hitler conquered Denmark, Norway, Holland, Belgium, and France.

Anti-Semitism in Poland

For twenty years before the invasion of Poland, Jewish life in Kraków had flourished socially, culturally, and economically, despite a long history of anti-Semitism that pervaded, or was spread throughout, Poland. In the years since Hitler had come to power in Germany in 1933, Polish anti-Semitism had become even more blatant, or obvious:

> Jewish businesses were often boycotted, pogroms were frequent, universities had segregated sections for Jews, and, in 1937, the Polish government supported an early Nazi plan to send all Jews to Madagascar.[42]

Consequently, at first many Poles welcomed the arrival of the German conquerors, not thinking about how their own freedom might eventually be affected. As one Jewish resident of Poland so wisely noted at the beginning of the Nazi takeover, many of the Polish people were "so happy to see full-scale persecution of Jews that they failed to see how it went hand in hand with a loss of freedom for everyone else."[43]

Yet the Nazis believed they were superior to all other people—not only the Jews, but to the non-Jewish Poles, as well. As Milton Meltzer explains, "The German soldiers entering Poland saw themselves as heroes of the 'master race'; their victims, the Poles, were Untermenschen, subhumans. And the Jews among them were an even lower category—bacilli."[44]

Consequently, the non-Jewish people of Poland were soon subjected to deporta-

---

To Save a Jew

Throughout World War II many Gentiles risked their lives to help save Jews. In The Samaritans: Heroes of the Holocaust, *authors Wladyslaw Bartoszewski and Zofia Lewin tell about the first Gentile killed in Poland while trying to save a Jew.*

"On September 6th, 1939, the day after the first German armored vehicles entered the town of Limanowa, nine Jews were arrested, kicked, insulted and thrown in waiting cars. The local postman, Jan Jakub Semik—not a Jew—tried to intervene, telling the Germans that those arrested were decent people. The Nazis ordered Semik to get into one of the cars and then drove off to the Cieniawa Woods near the village of Mordarka, where they shot him together with the Jews. Thus the first Pole to give his life in the defense of the Jews against the Nazis did so within less than a week of the invasion. His example was followed by many others."

Hans Frank (left), pictured with Italian minister of justice Count Dino Grani (middle) and the Reich's propaganda minister Joseph Goebbels (right), made it his mission to assist the Reich in eliminating all Jews from Poland.

tion themselves, often to Germany's slave-labor camps. At the same time, Poles were forcibly removed from their homes, and their businesses confiscated—both given to German Aryans.

Hans Frank and the New Order

After the fall of Poland the city of Kraków became the capital of what Hitler called the New Order of Poland. The newly created General Government was headed by

a man named Dr. Hans Frank—the epitome, or typical example, of a loyal Nazi leader, a man totally devoid of emotion or compassion for Jews. His goal, like Hitler's, was to rid Poland of all Jews. As he callously promised his associates at the end of his first year in office, "I could not eliminate all lice and Jews in only one year, but if you will help me, this end will be attained."[45]

Frank began his hideous mission on October 26, 1939, by issuing an order that required all Jewish males between the ages of fourteen and sixty to register for work for what was known as "on-call

A Jew wearing the required armband is stopped, searched, and questioned by the police.

forced labor." Many were immediately taken away to one of twelve forced-labor camps in the Kraków region, where they were forced to live and work under deplorable conditions. "Truly we are cattle in the eyes of the Nazis," wrote one Polish Jew in his diary at that time. "When they supervise Jewish workers they hold a whip in their hands. All are beaten unmercifully."[46]

Soon there were many other restrictions placed on everyday Jewish life. For example, Frank forbade the kosher preparation of food, and required all Jews to announce they were Jewish upon meeting someone new. Women were not allowed to have "hair-do's, wear short sleeves or high heels."[47]

In Warsaw, the capital of Poland, Jews were required to step off the sidewalk if they saw a German soldier coming in their direction, and in the town of Tomaszów Mazowiecki Jews were not allowed to be on the streets before eight o'clock in the morning or after twelve noon.

One month after the invasion all Jews had to turn in their radios, and a month and a half after that, on November 23, 1939, Frank issued a decree that required all Jewish men, women, and children over the age of ten to wear a white armband with a yellow Star of David on the left arm, so that they could be easily identified. Eventually a Jew who forgot to wear the armband could be hanged. There

Forced Labor

From 1939 until liberation in 1945, Jews were enslaved in what was called forced labor. Seymour Rossel describes forced labor in his book The Holocaust.

"Forced labor took many forms. Jews were rounded up in Poland, for example, and made to clean the streets, dig ditches, build canals and fortifications, and even build the walls of the Jewish ghettos—the very walls that held them prisoners. Jewish slaves were used to dig out huge plots of earth that served as mass graves when the Jews of a town were machine-gunned to death. In the death camps Jewish slaves were forced to move the bodies of dead Jews from the gas chambers to the furnaces where the bodies were burned, and to remove the ashes of the victims and clean the furnaces."

Much of the work that the Nazis forced upon the Jews was used as a way to dehumanize them. Here, Hitler Youth force Jews in Vienna to scrub the streets.

were also strict regulations against helping Jews:

> It was forbidden to have any kind of social intercourse [dealings] with Jews, or to add to their food rations, or to greet them or show other signs of courtesy—to mention only a few of the numerous, official pronouncements that regulated Jewish-German relations during those years.[48]

Despite these harsh injustices, in the early months of the occupation of Poland, most people felt that it would all be over soon and everything would get back to normal. Little did they know, however, that Hans Frank, like his führer, Adolf Hitler, had other plans for Jews throughout the New Order.

In Frank's diary entry for December 19, 1939, he chillingly wrote about the future of the Jews in Poland:

> The Jews represent for us extraordinarily malignant gluttons. We have now approximately 2,500,000 of them in the General Government and counting half-Jews, perhaps 3,500,000. We cannot shoot 2,500,000 Jews, neither can we poison them. We shall have to take steps, however, designed to extirpate [exterminate] them in some way—and this will be done.[49]

An Insane World—City of Opportunity

Oskar Schindler stepped into this insane world soon after the invasion of Poland. His arrival was, in many ways, like the blitzkrieg itself: sudden, swift, and overpowering.

Schindler, the opportunist and profiteer, had come to Kraków to seek his fortune. He saw a way to make a great deal of money as an industrialist contributing to the war effort. There was just one problem. He had little or no money to acquire the business that would make him rich. But he had something even better than money. He had what he himself might call panache, or flamboyant style; what others might call chutzpah, or supreme self-confidence—a combination of incredible nerve and unbelievable presumption.

Schindler also had one other trait that made him almost destined for success. It was a trait he had exhibited from the time he was a teenager: Schindler had a dynamic personality that could easily win people to his side or his point of view.

A Lifelong Friendship

Soon after arriving in Kraków Schindler met a man who would have a dramatic and lasting effect on his life. He was Itzhak Stern, a Jewish accountant.

Schindler first met Stern at the showroom of a fabric-manufacturing company called J. C. Buchheister, which Schindler thought he might try to acquire. Upon their meeting each other, something clicked, and the two unlikely friends—the scholarly Jew and the arrogant Gentile, or non-Jew—developed a friendship that lasted the rest of their lives. "Schindler, who fancied himself a deep thinker, enjoyed talking with and learning from Stern," says Eva Fogelman in her book *Conscience and Courage: Rescuers of Jews During the Holocaust*. "For his part, Stern, a member of the Zionist underground, judged

Schindler to be that rare breed, a 'good' German."[50] When Stern died in 1969, Schindler reportedly cried inconsolably.

Stern knew a great deal about the various businesses in Kraków, so he began to talk with Schindler about which ones were worth investigating for possible purchase and which ones were not. Finally Schindler asked the frail young accountant to take a look at the financial records of a company called Rekord, which made pots and pans, and which had recently been confiscated by the Germans from its Jewish owners. Schindler wondered what Stern thought about the company.

After carefully examining the company's financial statements, Stern pronounced it to be in good condition and put Schindler in touch with a Jewish businessman named Abraham Bankier. Bankier had many contacts with other Jew-ish men in Kraków who still had secret funds, despite the fact that Frank had confiscated all Jewish bank accounts, and who might be interested in investing in a new business venture.

By now these wealthy businessmen realized their money might soon be worthless or greatly reduced in value. It was more important to have tangible goods to trade, such as diamonds or gold or Persian rugs. They were willing to lend money to Schindler in return for a certain number of pots and pans each month, which they could in turn trade for the things they needed.

Thanks, then, to these Jewish investors, Schindler obtained the financial backing that made it possible for him to lease the factory from the Nazis and launch his new enamelware business by December 1939. Soon the suave, sophisticated, and outgoing

With financial help from Jewish investors, Schindler leased this enamelware factory in Kraków, a place that would become a safe haven for hundreds of his workers.

Oskar Schindler was known throughout Kraków as a successful businessman who entertained his high-ranking Nazi friends both lavishly and regularly. As a result, by early 1940 Schindler received his first important army contracts from the Armaments Inspectorate. This agency was charged with issuing contracts to manufacturing companies for the production of military equipment and supplies.

A Safe Haven

These new contracts helped Schindler acquire additional financing so that he could enlarge his plant and buy additional machinery. Soon he was employing more than 250 Poles, many of whom were Jews whom Itzhak Stern had asked Schindler to hire. Already word was spreading throughout the Jewish community that Oskar Schindler's factory was a safe haven—a place where Jews could be protected from the horrors that were now a daily occurrence.

As his business grew, Schindler also developed a lavish lifestyle, surrounding himself with all of the luxuries that life in war-torn Europe permitted. Always the handsome womanizer, he developed relationships with both a German woman named Ingrid and his Polish secretary, Victoria Klonowska. His wife, Emilie, who had remained at their home in Moravia while Schindler was building his career in Kraków, most likely knew about these affairs but clearly chose to ignore them. As she said years later, "He liked all women. You can fight against one but not against ten or a hundred women."[51]

Schindler, meanwhile, saw absolutely nothing wrong with his philandering. He never tried to hide his mistresses or to pretend they did not exist. "Oskar seems to have pursued his simultaneous attachments to three women and sundry casual friendships with others, all without suffering the normal penalties that beset the womanizer," according to Keneally.[52]

In the spring of 1940 Emilie came to visit her husband and stayed with him at his apartment on Straszewskiego Street

No Ordinary German

In this excerpt from The Book of the Just *by Eric Silver, Oskar Schindler proved to Itzhak Stern that he was not an anti-Semite.*

"When they introduced themselves, Schindler held out his hand. Stern declined to take it. When Schindler asked why, he explained that he was a Jew and it was forbidden for a Jew to shake a German's hand. Schindler answered with a Teutonic [Germanic] expletive: 'Scheisse.' Stern could tell from the start that this was no ordinary German."

Jewish men are rounded up and loaded onto trucks that will take them to forced-labor camps. At the time few imagined the atrocities that lay ahead.

throughout the summer, hoping, no doubt, that she and her husband could have the kind of committed relationship that most married couples enjoy. By fall, however, Emilie realized that her husband was not going to change. While she accepted his philandering, she did not want to live with it on a daily basis. So she returned to Moravia. As Keneally explains, "Emilie's intermittent relations with Oskar seem to have been those of a woman who knows her husband is not and will not be faithful, but who nonetheless doesn't want evidence of his affairs thrust under her nose."[53]

Free of Jews

By the time Emilie came to visit her husband in Kraków in the spring of 1940, many restrictions had been placed on the movement and activities of the Kraków Jews. They were banned, for example, from walking on the major streets of the city or from shopping in the major squares, and they were banned from public parks and concerts. That summer Hans Frank decided that there should be no Jews living in Kraków at all, since it was the capital of the New Order. So he issued a new decree that required all Jews to leave Kraków by August 1. He wanted Kraków to be Judenfrei (free of Jews), he said. Only Jews with special skills needed for the war effort would be allowed to remain in the city.

When Frank first announced this new edict, there were more than sixty thousand Jews still living in Kraków—nearly one-fourth of the total Kraków population of a quarter of a million people. By spring of 1941, forty thousand Jews had been expelled, forced to abandon their homes and businesses as they fled to Warsaw and other Polish cities. Soon the remaining twenty thousand Kraków Jews would be imprisoned in a ghetto in a southern section of the city.

Among the Jews who remained in Kraków were Schindler's factory workers, who now numbered more than one hundred. Yet now, as the snow began to fall in the closing months of 1940, the Nazis would often stop these workers as they were on their way to work in the morning and force them to shovel snow from the streets. Schindler complained to officials, stressing the fact that his workers were essential to the war effort and should not be detained on their way to the factory. As Keneally puts it:

> Oskar became an advocate of the principle that a factory owner should have unimpeded access to his own workers, that these workers should have access to the plant, that they should not be detained or tyrannized on their way to and from the factory.[54]

A Year of Contrasts

The year 1940 had been one of stark contrasts. For Schindler it had been a very good year. The brazen young tycoon had taken a nearly bankrupt manufacturing company and built it into an important new business for the war effort of Germany. He lived in a fancy apartment on an equally fancy street and spent money lavishly. He also developed important relationships and a high-profile public image that would help him and the Jews in his care to survive the difficult years ahead.

For the Jews in general, however, the year had been devastating and things promised to get worse. Thousands of families had been thrown out of their homes. Jewish businesses had been confiscated. Jewish children were no longer allowed to go to school. Jewish residents of Kraków were forbidden to ride trains without a special pass, and they were no longer allowed to have access to their bank accounts or safe-deposit boxes. Worse, they never knew when a truck might come in the night to take them away to a forced-labor camp, perhaps never to be heard from again.

Despite these injustices few Jews suspected the horrors that lay ahead. As Léon Poliakov explains in *Harvest of Hate: The Nazi Program for the Destruction of the Jews of Europe:*

> Cold-blooded extermination, so simple and so monstrous, went beyond their imagination; they expected ordeals, but firmly hoped to see them end. This is the first point to bear in mind in trying to understand what happened.[55]

As the year drew to an end, in an effort to console one another, Jews were often heard to say: "As long as things don't get any worse, we can live through this."

Things would, of course, get much worse.

Chapter

4 The Establishment of the Kraków Ghetto (1941)

On March 3, 1941, less than eighteen months after Oskar Schindler arrived in his adopted city of Kraków, Hans Frank issued a devastating new decree for the people of Kraków. He decided to make Kraków Judenfrei by establishing a Jewish ghetto—an area in Kraków where all Jews would have to reside. It was inconceivable, he said, that in the capital city of the New Order it was still necessary for Nazi officials to observe Jews on the streets of Kraków.

The deadline for entering the ghetto, which was to be located in a southern section of Kraków called Podgorze, was March 20, 1941. By that date all Aryans would have to move out of the designated area and all Jews—more than fifteen thousand out of an original Jewish population in Kraków of sixty thousand—would have to move in. Suddenly, Jews, whose ancestors had lived in Kraków for centuries, were prisoners in their own city.

The Ghettos of Poland

Kraków was not the first Polish city to establish a ghetto. Soon after Hitler invaded Poland, the city of Piotrków established a ghetto in October 1939. The following spring the city of Łódź established the first major ghetto in Poland, and that fall the largest Polish ghetto was established in Warsaw. All of these ghettos eventually extracted a devastating toll on human life through disease, starvation, or, more often, outright murder. In the Warsaw

Located in the poorest section of Poland, the Łódź ghetto provided horrendous living conditions for Jews. Misery, starvation, and death were rampant.

ghetto, for example, there were originally more than 550,000 people. By the time it was liquidated, or eliminated, only 45,000 people were left alive.

Throughout Poland these ghettos were located in the poorest or most rundown areas of the city, often on the outskirts of town and surrounded by high walls that the Nazis forced the Jews to build themselves. Inside the walled ghettos, which were like small, self-contained towns or villages, the living conditions were horrendous. Overcrowding was one problem. Small one- or two-room apartments often held two or more families. The lack of food was another problem. In Warsaw, for example, the inhabitants of the ghetto received fewer than two hundred calories per day. (By contrast, today in the United States the average teenager needs between twenty-two hundred and twenty-eight hundred calories a day.)

These miserable living conditions served a sinister purpose. As Ronnie S. Landau explains in his book *The Nazi Holocaust:*

The Nazis sought to create inhuman conditions in the ghettos, where a combination of obscene overcrowding, deliberate starvation, and outbreaks of typhus and cholera would reduce Jewish numbers through "natural wastage." Any Jew caught attempting to escape was to be shot on the spot.[56]

Homeless children struggle against hunger and cold on a Warsaw ghetto street.

The Germans established the Judenrat, a Jewish council that took orders directly from the Nazis.

Throughout the early weeks of March Schindler undoubtedly witnessed the steady migration of Jews into the Kraków ghetto. While many Jews had strenuously objected to the ghetto, others must have felt they would find some sense of security within its restricted confines. As Keneally explains:

> Although there was no great spontaneous joy among the Jews of Cracow as they packed for the move to Podgorze, there [was a] sense of arriving at a limit beyond which, with any luck, you wouldn't be further uprooted or tyrannized. Enough so that even some people from the villages around Cracow hurried to town lest they be locked out on March 20 and find themselves in a comfortless landscape.[57]

The Judenrat

In each of the ghettos throughout Poland, the Germans established a Judenrat, or Jewish council. The Judenrat, which consisted of a group of prominent members of the community, was responsible for governing the ghetto and handling all of the necessary administrative responsibilities. Its other functions, according to Malvina Graf, one of the prisoners of the Kraków ghetto, included "distributing food, allocating housing, assigning jobs, providing help to those without any means of support, keeping the Jewish section of the city clean, and administering hospitals and orphanages."[58]

The Nazis established the Judenrat to make the Jewish community think they were being governed by their own members. In truth the Judenrat took orders directly from the Nazis. Often this meant that the Judenrat had to participate in the selection of people for deportation. The Nazis, Meltzer says, used "this pretense of self-government as a device to get the Jews to cooperate in their own extermination. It was a fiendishly clever idea to put the blame for their own degradation and destruction upon the Jews themselves."[59]

Seven months after the Kraków ghetto was established, the Nazis issued a new order on October 15, 1941. This one forbade Jews to leave the ghetto under penalty of death. At the same time, any person who was caught trying to hide or help a Jew escape from the ghetto was also subject to the death penalty. Suddenly signs appeared throughout Kraków, with an ominous warning to all Polish gentiles: "Whoever helps Jews," the signs said, "will be punished by death."

Life in the Ghetto

Although Aryans, or non-Jews, were not permitted to live in the ghetto, a small number were permitted to continue their businesses there. A pharmacy called Under the Eagle, run by a Polish gentile named Tadeusz Pankiewicz, was one. For nearly two and a half years Pankiewicz watched the devastation and human destruction as it took place in the town square, called Plac Zgody, located in front of his pharmacy. The Polish word *plac* means "harmony," or "peace." Ironically—almost perversely—Plac Zgody soon proved to be anything but harmonious or peaceful.

After the war Pankiewicz wrote a book called *The Cracow Ghetto Pharmacy*, recounting in detail what he observed during those tragic years. As he puts it, during the years of the Kraków ghetto, there were "inhuman deportations, monstrous crimes and the constant degradation of human dignity and self-respect of the occupants."[60]

Despite these unbelievable hardships the prisoners of the ghetto struggled to carry on as much of a normal life as possible under such abnormal circumstances.

They continued to provide education for the children in secret, health care for those who needed it, secret religious services, and even some social activities. Writing about those days, one survivor of the Kraków ghetto said:

> In order to develop economic independence in the ghetto, a number of stores, cafes, restaurants, and other small businesses were opened. One could even find entertainment in the restaurants, with dancing and performances by local artists. There was even an orchestra, which was conducted by the violinist Rosner, assisted by his brother, who was a pianist.[61]

The Deadly *Aktions*

But the instability and uncertainty of life in the ghetto soon became apparent. Beginning in the fall of 1941 the Nazis began to periodically remove people from the ghetto. Usually without warning the Nazis would storm into the ghetto and indiscriminately round up a group of people who, they claimed, were to be resettled. These sudden roundups, which initially focused on the old and unemployed or the sick, were known as *Aktions*.

At first these *Aktions* seemed to many residents to make sense, or at least to be understandable. The authorities convinced them that deportees were being resettled in order to provide better, even safer, living conditions for the rest of the ghetto's residents. Soon, however, the Nazis began rounding up people purely at random. At about the same time, rumors began to spread that the residents were

Jews gather their belongings before boarding a train that will deport them to a concentration camp.

not being resettled at another ghetto, but instead were being deported to concentration camps or even taken outside the ghetto for immediate mass execution.

Suddenly, throughout the ghetto everyone lived in fear of being selected for transport. The day-to-day brutality of the Nazis toward the Jews increased. Malvina Graf remembers the horror of those days in her book, *The Krakow Ghetto and the Plaszow Camp Remembered:*

> SS men passing in the ghetto streets attacked and kicked Jews at random. They would frequently grab elderly re-

ligious Jewish men and shave their sidelocks and beards, all the while making vicious jokes.[62]

Schindler's Workers

During this time Jews with proper identification cards—a yellow card called a *Kennkarte*, which had their photographs and a large J, for Jude, stamped on it—were allowed to continue working outside the ghetto. Every day armed guards would

Life in the Kraków Ghetto

Malvina Graf, a survivor of the Kraków ghetto, tells about day-to-day life during the early days of the ghetto in her book The Krakow Ghetto and the Plaszow Camp Remembered.

"Gradually, hospitals, orphanages, old-age homes, and a post office (using special stamps for Jews) were established in the ghetto; also a bath house and an Entlausung (delousing center) were opened. Formal education was forbidden, but secret schools were opened, with children gathering in private homes for instruction. The practice of religion was also banned, but religious activities did not cease; in fact, three synagogues were secretly established in the ghetto. Jews were becoming accustomed to the new way of life; many learned to cope, and there was no outward loss of motivation, even though many worked long and hard hours with little, if any, reward."

Boys sit on the curb of a busy ghetto street. Though schooling was forbidden, secret schools were created to educate young Jews.

German, Polish, and Jewish workers at Schindler's enamelware factory in Kraków. Unlike most non-Jews, Schindler showed compassion toward his Jewish workers at a time when a person could be arrested or even sentenced to death for helping Jews.

march these workers to the factories where they were employed, such as Schindler's enamelware factory, and then march them back to the ghetto at night. According to Graf:

> Wearing armbands on their coat-sleeves and carrying their Kennkarten, thousands of people passed through the gates to their jobs in the city, while those who did not have jobs, or were old and sick, remained behind the ghetto walls.[63]

Until now Schindler had paid his Jewish workers a minimal amount of money for their labor. Beginning on March 20, 1941, however, all factory owners were ordered to pay the wages or fees for their workers directly to the SS. "Jews were from then on expected to live on nothing but their rations, which were totally insufficient to sustain health."[64]

Schindler went out of his way to take good care of the Jews who worked at DEF, often calling on his legendary charm and ingratiating, or flattering, manner to help his workers get out of difficult situations. Once, says author Eric Silver in *The Book of the Just,*

> two Gestapo men came to his office and demanded that he hand over a family of five who had bought forged Polish identity papers. "Three hours after they walked in," Schindler [said] . . . "two drunken Gestapo men reeled out of my office without their prisoners and without the incriminating documents they had demanded."[65]

A Deadly *Aktion*

Tadeusz Pankiewicz was the only non-Jewish Pole allowed to live inside the Kraków ghetto in the district of Podgorze. From his pharmacy he observed the June 1942 Aktion, *which is described in this excerpt from his book* The Cracow Ghetto Pharmacy.

"The Ghetto echoed with shots; the dead and wounded fell; blood marked the German crimes in the streets. There were more and more people in the square. The heat, as on previous days, was unbearable—fire seemed to fall from the sky. Water was unavailable, but even if it were, it was forbidden to the sufferers. People, weakened by heat and thirst, fainted and fell. Every few minutes the SS men brought valises filled with valuables taken during the searches of the deportees. They took everything from them: rings, wedding bands, gold and steel watches, cigarette cases and even lighters. Some of the unfortunates looked at those waiting their turn, resignation and apathy etched in their faces. These people were already beyond feeling."

Schindler also extended basic human kindness to the Jews, something few people cared or even dared to do at this time. He would bring them extra food, although this was strictly forbidden by the Nazis, and found ways to provide his Jewish workers with other things that they normally could not have, such as cigarettes. "He would smoke a lot in the factory," says Ester Kaufman, one of the Jewish survivors who worked at Emalia, the name the Jewish workers often called Schindler's factory. "He would take one puff and throw it on the ground, then light another and do the same thing. That was the only way he could give us cigarettes."[66]

Years later almost every one of Schindler's workers remembered some small kindness he had extended to them. Once, according to Moshe Bejski, one of

Schindler's workers broke his glasses and could not see. Schindler replaced them. In another instance a mother, who had hidden her child with a Christian family in Poland, was desperate to know if the child was well. Schindler managed to bring a message from the child to his mother. On another occasion a worker was ill and simply wanted an apple. Schindler brought it to her.

These small, seemingly insignificant acts of kindness were, on the contrary, extremely significant in view of the fact that to show any kind of compassion for Jews at that time was against the law. A person could be arrested, imprisoned, or even sentenced to death for helping Jews in any way.

Schindler also reportedly began to smuggle children out of the ghetto, delivering them to Polish nuns who either hid them from the Nazis or claimed they were Christian orphans. "This was an act of compassion," says psychotherapist and author Wundheiler, "deepened and enhanced by Schindler's identification with the children as well as their parents."[67]

Schindler did one other thing for the Jews that no one else dared to do. It was, perhaps, the most important thing anyone could give the victims of such outrageous hatred and injustice. He gave them hope. He gave them hope by constantly reassuring them that they would be safe and would survive the war as long as they continued to work in his factory.

The Final Solution

Those must have been comforting words. Yet at the same time, Hitler and the other leaders of the Nazi Party were already discussing the Final Solution, Hitler's term for the systematic murder of all Jews. Years earlier Hitler had talked about shipping all Jews to the island of Madagascar, in the Indian Ocean. That plan was rejected but the ultimate goal remained. A high-level German official quoted Hitler as saying:

The Jewish question [must] be solved once and for all. The Jews are the

A woman lies dead on a ghetto street, a victim of hunger and exposure. Even though inhumane conditions in the ghettos already caused thousands of Jews to die, the deaths were not enough for Hitler, who planned to carry out what he called the Final Solution, the systematic murder of all Jews.

Resistance

In his book
Schindler's List,
*Thomas Keneally
describes the various
acts of resistance that
were carried out in
Kraków by the young
Zionists of the Halutz
Youth and the ZOB,
Jewish Combat
Organization, during
1942.*

"In [the SS-reserved Cyganeria Restaurant in Kraków] they left a bomb which blew the tables through the roof, tore seven SS men to fragments, and injured some forty more. When Oskar heard about it, he knew he could have been there, buttering up some official. The ZOB would in a few months sink patrol boats on the Vistula, fire-bomb sundry military garages throughout the city, arrange Passiercheins [special passes] for people who were not supposed to have them, smuggle passport photographs out to centers where they could be used in the forging of Aryan papers, derail the elegant Army-only train that ran between Cracow and Bochnia, and get their underground newspaper into circulation."

sworn enemies of the German people and must be eradicated. Every Jew that we can lay our hands on is to be destroyed now during the war, without exception.[68]

Later that same year, on December 16, 1941, Hans Frank gave another speech condemning the Jews to death: "Gentlemen, I must ask you to rid yourself of all feelings of pity. We must annihilate the Jews wherever we find them and wherever it is possible, in order to maintain here the integral [essential] structure of the Reich."[69]

In January 1942 fourteen German officials—eight of whom were highly educated, holding doctoral degrees, and all of whom were elite members of the Nazi Party—met at a villa in Wannsee, a suburb of Berlin, to discuss the Jewish question. Within ninety minutes they had all enthusiastically agreed to Hitler's Final Solution—the systematic murder of eleven million Jews.

No one, of course, will ever be able to adequately explain how these supposedly intelligent, cultured men could have had such total disregard for human life. No one will ever be able to explain how they could possibly agree to annihilate every single Jew on the continent of Europe.

5 No Exceptions; No Mercy: The Turning Point (1942)

On April 28, 1942, Oskar Schindler celebrated his thirty-fourth birthday. From all accounts it was a festive occasion for this young entrepreneur whose business, by now, was one of the many success stories of the New Order.

Schindler celebrated with a party at his suburban factory on Lipowa Street in Zablocie, where he undoubtedly thanked his Jewish workers for their labor. Amid the gaiety that spring day, Schindler impulsively kissed a young Jewish girl on the cheek.

The next morning the Gestapo arrived at Schindler's factory to arrest him for racial improprieties. According to the Race and Resettlement Act, it was considered a crime for an Aryan to have any relations with a Jew, including the offering of a fatherly kiss on the cheek.

Schindler (top, left) celebrates his thirty-fourth birthday with local SS officials. The same day he would be arrested and sent to prison for kissing a young Jewish girl on the cheek.

Schindler was put in prison. It was not the first time he had been arrested by the Gestapo. At the end of 1941 he was arrested, presumably for his dealings on the black market. Before he was taken away, he gave his secretary a list of influential men to call who could help him. That time he was detained only overnight. By morning many high-placed Nazi officials had called the low-level Gestapo agent in Kraków, and Schindler was released with an apology.

This time Schindler remained in jail for five days before his influential friends in the Nazi Party were able to get him released. He must have thought during this time, if only briefly, that even he was not entirely protected from the scourge of the Nazis. He must have wondered just how long even the popular Oskar Schindler, with his influential friends and his generous gifts, could escape the brutal Nazi retribution, or punishment, for something so simple and natural as caring for other human beings.

A Bold Rescue

In 1942 all residents of the Kraków ghetto had to obtain a new identification card, called a *Blauschein*, a "blue card." Only those who could find useful employment could obtain a *Blauschein*, however. The card identified a person as an essential worker. Those who did not have the *Blauschein* could be arrested.

On the morning of June 3, 1942, Abraham Bankier, Schindler's office manager, was preparing to leave the ghetto to go to work at DEF in Zablocie when the Gestapo demanded to see his *Blauschein*. Suddenly he realized that he did not have this vitally important card—a card that could spell the difference between life and death.

Moments later Bankier, along with dozens of other Jews from the Kraków ghetto, was marched to the train station. They were crammed into boxcars like unwanted cattle, where they then waited to be taken to a forced-labor camp. Fortunately an associate of Schindler's saw Bankier being taken away and immediately notified Schindler of what was taking place.

Schindler rushed to the train station and, standing face-to-face with a young Nazi officer, demanded that the prisoners be released. With all the casual bravado he could muster, he hinted that if Bankier and the others were not released immediately, the young officer would soon find himself in southern Russia.

Bankier was released. But the episode left a disturbing impression on Schindler. For almost three years he had witnessed the brutality that the Nazis inflicted on the Jews of Kraków and had heard about people being forcibly taken from their homes and families for deportation. Yet hearing about the deportations and actually witnessing one firsthand were two different things. As Keneally explains, "It was the first time Oskar had seen this juxtaposition [side-by-side placement] of humans and cattle cars, and it was a greater shock than hearing of it."[70]

A Horrifying *Aktion*

"*Alle Heraus!*" the Germans shouted, as hundreds of special guards raced through the streets of the Kraków ghetto on the morning of June 8, 1942. "*Schnell—Raus!*"

Armed Nazi soldiers herd Jews toward the deportation trains during the final liquidation of the Warsaw ghetto in 1943.

they demanded, ordering everybody to gather quickly at Plac Zgody for the beginning of one of the most deadly *Aktions* that had yet occurred in the ghetto.

Thousands of ghetto residents poured onto the square as the processing of deportees began. "There was widespread panic," one victim later recalled, "and the only topic discussed concerned the possibility of being selected for transport."[71]

From inside his pharmacy, Tadeusz Pankiewicz watched the shocking events take place:

> The Ghetto reverberated with shots. Soldiers were running amok with smoking rifles, officers with pistols, pokers, clubs and whips. The corpses and wounded were removed by the hospital orderlies, making their way through the crowd under constant fire. The Germans shot as if possessed, at random, at whosoever satisfied their whim. Apparently, blood exacerbated [intensified] their bestial and sadistic instincts.[72]

A Disturbing Vantage Point

Early that morning Schindler and his mistress, Ingrid, had decided to go riding in the hills above the ghetto. Hearing the noise from below, they reined their horses to a stop to watch the horrifying events of this terrifying June *Aktion* unfold.

At first transfixed by the indiscriminate slaughter of human life, Schindler finally moved away from the view of the ghastly executions and torture. It was then, according to Keneally, that Schindler suddenly and completely realized the deadly seriousness of the Nazis' resolve. He realized he was watching "a statement of his government's policy which could not be written off as a temporary aberration. The SS men were, Oskar believed, fulfilling there the orders of the leader."[73]

The Meaning of Deportation

In The Cracow Ghetto Pharmacy *Tadeusz Pankiewicz tells about a letter he received from someone who had escaped from the ghetto and traveled through the town of Belzec. The letter, he says, was the "first authentic confirmation" of the fate of deportees.*

"The author described realistically the trains filled with people, stationed in Belzec for days awaiting destination orders. This meant moving the transport to a side branch of the railroad ending in a deep woods surrounded by fences and barbed wire. The area over the forest was enveloped in thick smoke, and an unusual noxious odor pervaded the air. The deportees who lived through the ghastliness of the transport in the closed [cattle] cars remained for days at the [train station at Belzec] without a drop of water or a morsel of food. Moans and cries for help came from the cars, but assistance was forbidden. German police guarded the train. When it arrived in the woods, the guards opened the doors, and those still alive had to strip and were herded into gas chambers; then their bodies were cremated, and so the smoke hung heavily over the area. The letter ended with an appeal that no one be deceived about the fate of the deportees."

Now Schindler knew the truth. There were to be no exceptions, no mercy. Hitler planned to annihilate all Jews. "Beyond this day," Schindler later said, "no thinking person could fail to see what would happen. I was now resolved to do everything in my power to defeat the system."[74]

A Tale of Horrors

After every deportation rumors slowly filtered back to the ghetto about the fate of the loved ones who had been torn from them. Some said they had been transported to forced-labor camps; others imagined secret Nazi factories. Yet no one wanted to believe the ultimate horror. "In spite of everything, the thought of mass murders, gas chambers and crematoria was not yet conceivable."[75]

But that summer Schindler—as well as the residents of the ghetto—received news that began to convince them of the atrocities that were taking place throughout Poland. A young dentist named Bachner had been shipped off during the June *Aktion* to Belzec, a concentration camp that Schindler had undoubtedly heard about. Somehow Bachner had managed to escape by slipping into a latrine, where he stood for two days in human waste.

Eventually he found his way back to the ghetto, where he told the residents the truth about what was happening. He told them that there were camps where hundreds, perhaps thousands, of people were sent to gas chambers every day and then cremated. In *Schindler's List*, Keneally dramatically retells the story Bachner must have told his friends and family throughout the ghetto about what he observed at the Belzec death camp:

> The people were lined up in front of two large warehouses, one marked "Cloak Room" and the other "Valuables." The new arrivals were made to

Heaps of prisoners' clothing are a shocking reminder of those who died at Dachau.

Prisoners at Dachau concentration camp. Once arriving here few prisoners survived the harsh conditions. If they were not shot or sent to the gas chambers, they were starved or worked to death.

> undress, and a small Jewish boy passed among the crowd handing out lengths of string with which to tie their shoes together. Spectacles and rings were removed. So, naked, the prisoners had their heads shaved in the hairdresser's, an SS NCO [noncommissioned officer] telling them that their hair was needed to make something special for U-boat [submarine] crews. It would grow again, he said, maintaining the myth of their continued usefulness. At last the victims were driven down a barbed-wire passage to bunkers which had copper Stars of David on their roofs and were labeled "Baths and Inhalation Rooms." SS men reassured them all the way, telling them to breathe deeply, that it was an excellent means of disinfection.

Bachner saw a little girl drop a bracelet on the ground, and a boy of three picked it up and went into the bunker playing with it. In the bunkers, said Bachner, they were all gassed.[76]

As residents of the ghetto listened to this story of incomprehensible horror, they would have been incredulous, or unbelieving. How could anyone believe such tales of insanity? Germany was a cultured, civilized society, they argued. No civilized society could suddenly become so despicably barbaric. No civilized human being could possibly stomach, let alone participate in, the slaughter of so many other human beings, they insisted. As Tadeusz Pankiewicz later expressed it, it was impossible that "in the twentieth century any nation could sink so low."[77]

Slowly that fearful summer the residents of the Kraków ghetto and other ghettos throughout Poland began to comprehend just how low, indeed, a nation could sink, as finally, they began to grasp the full extent of the human devastation that was taking place.

The Jewish Relief Organization

In December 1942 an agent from a Zionist rescue organization in Budapest, the capital of Hungary, came to see Schindler in Kraków. The organization had heard, perhaps from Itzhak Stern, that Schindler

---

No Longer to Ask Why

In the years since the Holocaust many people have asked why the Jews did not resist the horrors that confronted them. Tadeusz Pankiewicz offers one explanation in his book The Cracow Ghetto Pharmacy.

"Anyone who did not see at first hand the awesome horror could not understand or grasp the dire circumstances that plagued these people. They could not fathom the perfidious [treacherous] lies which misled them the day before their death. If my questioners could spend even a few hours in the funereal atmosphere in which these Aktions took place. . . . At every few steps someone was killed, beaten, humiliated and tortured. If one could look behind the scenes of these crimes and see the perpetrators, observe the means they used to instill fear and terror, cruelly shooting, and deceiving the 'resettled' with a hope that they would live; if the inquirers knew about the threats of revenge on the entire family for even thinking about escape, for sabotage, and for any self-defense action—he would no longer ask 'why.'"

Inmates were forced to construct the camps where they or their own people would die. Here, prisoners pull carts loaded with stones to construct roads through the camp at Plaszow.

could be trusted and might be willing to provide the organization with firsthand information about the crimes that were going on in the Kraków ghetto and throughout Poland. Schindler agreed; so in December 1942 he sneaked out of Poland in the baggage car of a train, hidden beneath newspaper.

In a hotel in Budapest Schindler met with a small group of men, providing them with the first eyewitness account of the events in Kraków. In a somber tone, Schindler told the men that every day more and more people were being taken out of the ghetto. Some were sent to forced-labor camps. But many others were sent to newly constructed camps that the SS called *Vernichtungslagers*, "extermination camps." According to Keneally:

> The Vernichtungslagers also used people as labor for a time, but their ultimate industry was death and its by-products—the recycling of the clothes, of remaining jewelry or spectacles, of toys, and even of the skin and hair of the dead.[78]

Schindler also told the rescue organization about a new forced-labor camp that was being built on the sacred grounds of an old Jewish cemetery in Plaszow, an area on the outskirts of Kraków. Every day Jewish prisoners were being tortured and murdered in the construction of this camp. At the same time they were ordered to use the tombstones from the cemetery to pave the roads through the camp, desecrating, or violating, the graves of their ancestors. It was now only a matter of time, Schindler told the committee, before the Kraków ghetto would be liquidated and the Jews imprisoned in this new camp.

Having finished giving this startling testimony in Budapest, Schindler returned to Kraków with a suitcase full of money to pass to the Jewish underground leaders. In the coming months he would pass additional sums of money to the underground. He would also be "asked repeatedly—and this was a far riskier assignment—to request transfers of Jews from deadly forced-labor camps to his benign factory."[79] It was a request that Schindler would never fail to tackle aggressively.

6 "An Hour of Life Is Still Life": Establishing a Camp at Plaszow (1943)

On February 13, 1943, SS captain Amon Leopold Goeth took charge of the final construction of the Plaszow camp and the liquidation of the Kraków ghetto. A tall, handsome man, forty-year-old Goeth would soon prove to be one of the most sadistic savages among all the SS—more vicious than his two dogs, Rolf and Ralf, who "had been trained to attack Jews on command."[80]

By now the Kraków ghetto had been divided into two sections: Ghetto A consisted of about ten thousand relatively healthy men and women who would soon be forced to work at the factories of Plaszow; Ghetto B consisted of two thousand people who were scheduled to receive "special treatment." In truth they were to be sent to Auschwitz for extermination because they were considered useless to the needs of the camp. This group included many women and children, as well as the sick and elderly.

As word spread about the coming liquidation, many residents discussed how they might escape. Leopold Pfefferberg and his wife, Ludmilla, talked about trying to escape through the sewers. They had heard about others who had made their escape from the ghetto this way, wading in rat-infested filth as they desperately made their way to freedom. But they also knew

that the SS could easily be waiting to gun them down as they came out of the sewer on the other end, so they did not make the escape attempt.

The Last Day of the Kraków Ghetto

Schindler had learned that the day for the final liquidation of the Kraków ghetto was scheduled for March 13, 1943. So on the night of March 12, in order to protect his workers from what was certain to be a bloody *Aktion* the next day, he made them stay at the factory. "Schindler told us not to return to the ghetto as we would normally do," remembers Sol Urbach, a teenager at the time, "but to remain there and make the best of it by sleeping wherever we could because there was trouble in the ghetto. The ghetto was being liquidated and there were killings going on."[81]

The Kraków ghetto's last day began at dawn. As the SS marched through the gates into the ghetto, the residents were ordered to gather at Plac Zgody in preparation for their march to Plaszow. Those who attempted to hide were rousted from their hiding places and often shot on the spot.

A Jewish police officer patrols a ghetto street. Rumors about deportation and its terrible consequences filled ghetto residents with fear.

As with previous *Aktions*, hundreds of people were beaten or murdered in cold blood. Says Pankiewicz, who watched the human destruction from inside his pharmacy:

> The only difference was that this time the murdering was greatly increased, as if for the finale the Germans wanted to sate [gorge] themselves in blood. The shooting from early morning was incessant. Everyone who wanted to shoot did so.[82]

As hundreds of people lay dead in the streets, the Nazis ordered a group of Jews to strip the dead of all clothing and to load the bodies onto trucks to be transported to mass graves outside of Kraków. Years later Moshe Pantirer, one of the survivors of the liquidation of the ghetto, still painfully remembers coming across a young boy who was badly wounded, but not yet dead. "We asked a German if he would shoot the boy out of kindness so we wouldn't have to bury him alive. But the German answered no. 'He's not worth wasting a bullet on,'" Pantirer recalled sadly.[83]

By the end of the day seven centuries of Jewish life in Kraków had been wiped out, eliminated as if it had never existed. Goeth had finally achieved Hans Frank's original objective of making Kraków Judenfrei. In the process, according to survivor Graf,

> entire families had been destroyed and, with them, a tradition of Jewish life that had survived even the worst of times for Jews in the history of Poland—families whose members had, over the centuries, left a lasting impact on all that spoke of culture, all that spoke of the humanities in Poland.[84]

During the liquidation, many Kraków Jews were murdered outright. Thousand of others were sent to an extermination camp at Birkenau, one of six such death camps in Poland, where they ultimately were sent to the gas chambers. The rest were sent to the newly constructed forced-labor camp at Plaszow.

The Monster, Goeth

In her book The Krakow Ghetto and the Plaszow Camp Remembered, *Malvina Graf, imprisoned at Plaszow as a teenager, tells about the terrifying commandant, Amon Goeth.*

"Shooting a human being was a trivial matter to Amon Goeth. Often, he would look up from the meal he was eating and, displeased with what he saw (it could be the weather), would unholster his gun and fire into the group of workers. Thus mollified, he would survey his handiwork—loose, shapeless masses crumpled on the ground, in sharp contrast to the living, moving trickle [of blood] that seeped into the snow, staining it crimson—and nod as if satisfied, reholster his gun, and turn back to his meal."

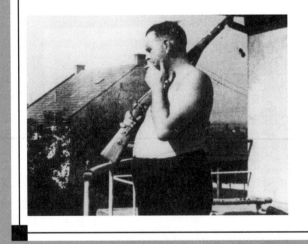

Amon Goeth, a terrifyingly sadistic SS captain, was in charge of the final liquidation of the Kraków ghetto.

Years later Schindler would still talk about the horror of what he saw that day with utter disbelief and astonishment that such a cruel and inhuman event could take place. Many survivors believe that the horrors he observed the day the Kraków ghetto was liquidated totally turned Schindler against the Nazis. "When he witnessed the liquidation of the ghetto and saw the brutalities firsthand," says one survivor, "he changed his mind about the Nazis. He decided to get out and to save as many Jews as he could."[85] He must have realized at that moment that with the liquidation of the Kraków ghetto went any shred of hope that the Jews might be saved—unless he alone took action to save them.

The Plaszow Camp

Its official name was the SS and Kraków District Police Forced Labor Camp. Regardless of what it was called, however, the Plaszow camp was a nightmare beyond description. Sol Urbach remembers:

> Even as a youngster of 15, I knew that I had entered into hell when I walked into that camp. The gallows were there in the open. People were being shot randomly. There was smoke from the places where bodies were being burned.[86]

In Plaszow there was a main square called the *Appelplatz*. This was a frightening place—a place where Jews were assembled every morning for roll call; a place where Jews were selected for deportation; a place where Jews were humiliated, tortured, and murdered. During the year and a half that this camp was in operation, a total of 150,000 prisoners passed through the *Appelplatz*; more than 80,000 of them were killed there. Says author Shmuel Krakowski:

> Their fate was completely in the hands of the camp's command staff, guards, and clerks, whose harshness towards the prisoners knew no limit. Any prisoner was liable to suffer the cruelest of tortures, or the worst possible death for any offense and for any inoffense, for that matter.[87]

A Vicious Killer

Soon everyone in camp knew just how vicious and cruel Goeth could be. He would kill indiscriminately, depending on his mood or whim at any given moment. Henry Wermeuth was one of the prisoners at Plaszow who witnessed Goeth's barbaric actions:

> You never knew from day to day whether or not the whim of that monster Goeth would bring about your death. Death would come by pure chance. It was like being in a pen from which the farmer selects beasts for the slaughter willy-nilly. Plaszow was the worst time for me, because of the tension.[88]

Plaszow prisoners carry food to others laying railroad tracks.

In her book *The Krakow Ghetto and the Plaszow Camp Remembered*, Malvina Graf also tells about many of Goeth's brutal and gruesome murders. For example, one day a young girl named Zosia and her mother were working in the quarry as Goeth rode by on his horse. He stopped and got off and showed the mother how to use the hammer correctly to split stones. He then calmly took out his gun and shot the woman in the head. Says Graf:

> When her mother fell to the ground, lifeless, Zosia, who was right there, could not say a single word, because she, too, would then be killed. Only after Goeth went away could she shed her bitter tears. Hardly a day passed without an occurrence of this sort.[89]

Early in his reign of terror over the Plaszow camp, Goeth met with Schindler and other local manufacturers to talk with them about moving their factories inside the camp. According to Keneally, he explained to these successful entrepreneurs that there were

> mutual advantages of moving an industry inside the camp perimeter. The factory owners did not have to pay for the premises, and he, the Commandant, did not have to provide a guard to march the prisoners to town and back.[90]

Schindler, hoping to keep his Jewish employees as far from harm as possible, was totally against the idea. Exhibiting his skill as a diplomat, Schindler explained to Goeth that he had important war contracts that had to be fulfilled in a timely manner. Moving the machinery to Plaszow would simply take too long, and it would interfere with his contribution to the war effort.

A few days later Schindler heard about one of the first executions at Plaszow—the murder of a young woman who was an engineer and architect. Goeth summarily ordered her execution because one of the walls to a building she had been supervising had collapsed. Hearing about this execution strengthened Schindler's resolve to keep his workers out of Plaszow and away from the murderous Goeth and his men—no matter how much it would cost him to do so.

Whether through his innate, or inborn, charm or through a generous gift to Goeth—perhaps both—Schindler was granted permission to maintain his factory outside the Plaszow camp in the suburb of Zablocie. Each day, until the liquidation of

When Schindler (shown here at his factory) heard about the atrocities at Plaszow, he resolved to keep his workers out of the camp.

A Race for Death

In his book The Cracow Ghetto Pharmacy, *Tadeusz Pankiewicz describes many gruesome scenes of physical and mental torture during the final liquidation of the ghetto. In this excerpt he describes a diabolical race for death.*

"The SS men started to line up the crowd facing the exits, separating the women from the men, taking the children from their mothers. All this was done with unbelievable cruelty and inhumanity. Like the sadists they were, beatings, and murders apparently stimulated their eagerness for new thrills. They arranged a race of death. They selected people and placed them in groups. They were told to run forward as fast as they could. The outcome, they were told, would decide whether they lived or died. Amid jeering and laughter, the wretched victims ran, at first individually, then in groups. The SS men shot at them. The fast ones saved themselves temporarily. The SS men patted them on their shoulders, praised them for their fast pace and for their good condition and endurance, then ordered them to turn round and shot them in the back of the head."

Plaszow, his forced-labor workers were marched under heavy guard from Plaszow to Emalia and returned to Plaszow at night.

Children at Plaszow

Goeth issued an order that no children under the age of thirteen were allowed at the camp. On the final day of the Kraków ghetto, when the prisoners were led into Plaszow, the SS watched carefully for any children whose parents might try to smuggle them into the camp. "Children who were detected were brutally torn away from their parents."[91]

One eight-year-old who was smuggled into the camp tried to blend in with the older boys at the brush factory where he worked. "It was like a terrible adventure," he later recalled, "where the winning position was staying alive."[92]

Goeth lived in a large villa at Plaszow, where he entertained guests frequently, including Oskar Schindler. Remembering those days, Helen Rosenzweig, one of Goeth's servants at the time, told a reporter about frequently seeing Schindler at the villa with Goeth. "A few times I saw him with his wife, Emilie Schindler, who was a very quiet, subdued, refined-looking lady," Rosenzweig said. "But many times he would come with other women and stay on the top floor of the villa."[93]

During this time many survivors remember the kindnesses Schindler extended to them. "My mother was ill and

Schindler (second from left) with his workers at the enamelware factory. To keep his workers from the daily beatings and killings at Plaszow, Schindler convinced Nazi officials to allow him to build a subcamp so his workers could live and work at his factory.

he brought me medication for her," Rosenzweig continued. "And one time he brought me silk stockings. I think he felt sorry for me."[94]

Goeth believed that he and the gregarious, fun-loving Schindler were friends. The truth was that Schindler found Goeth repugnant. Yet Schindler knew that it was to his advantage to be viewed as a friend and confidant of this murderous villain, so he made Goeth feel that they were like brothers. It was all an act—and a good one at that. Says Thomas Keneally:

> Oskar had the characteristic salesman's gift of treating men he abhorred as if they were spiritual brothers. But from the evidence of Stern and others it is obvious that, from the time of their earlier contacts, Oskar abominated Goeth as a man who went to the work of murder as calmly as a clerk goes to his office.[95]

Schindler's Subcamp

As Schindler learned more about the daily beatings and killings of the prisoners in Plaszow, he resolved to take a more positive step to protect his workers. He decided to set up dormitories at his factory so that his workers could sleep at Emalia and not have to undergo the exhausting marches between Plaszow and Zablocie. They also would not be subjected to the daily beatings and killings that went on at Plaszow.

At first Goeth objected to this plan. But Schindler, again using his unique power of persuasion, convinced Goeth that this arrangement would be far more productive for the war effort. As he explained it, he could get more work out of his laborers since they would not have to spend time traveling between Plaszow and his plant in Zablocie.

The Plaszow Camp Security

Shmuel Krakowski describes the physical characteristics of the Plaszow camp in his book The War of the Doomed: Jewish Resistance in Poland.

"This camp was isolated from the outside world by a triple barrier—an electric fence, a special barbed-wire fence, and a regular barbed-wire fence. There were fifteen additional barriers made of iron wire inside the camp, separating its various parts, while the main section of prisoner barracks was separated from the rest of the camp by an additional electric fence. There were three kinds of watch towers in and around the camp: towers two meters high were placed every twenty meters, for supervising the various parts of the camp and guarding the internal barriers which prevented the movement of prisoners from one section to another; towers five to eight meters high were stationed around the outside fence of the camp and equipped with installations for heavy machine guns, telephones, and alarm systems, and towers fifteen meters high overlooked the entire camp."

Jewish women on their way to forced labor march past the menacing barbed wire and electric fencing surrounding the Plaszow camp.

So it was agreed that Schindler's factory could become an SS forced-labor subcamp—under one condition. It would have to follow strict guidelines for the construction of a subcamp. This, Keneally says,

> involved the erection of fences nine feet tall, of watchtowers at given intervals according to the length of the camp perimeter, of latrines, barracks, a clinic, a dental office, a bathhouse and delousing complex, a barbershop, a good store, a laundry, a barracks office, a guard block of somewhat better construction than the barracks themselves, and all the accessories.[96]

Schindler agreed to these conditions and paid for the enormous costs of constructing such a camp himself.

Schindlerjuden

Although they were still prisoners, the inmates at Schindler's subcamp felt that they had arrived in paradise, as compared to the Plaszow camp. By now they referred to themselves, almost reverently, as Schindlerjuden, "Schindler's Jews," undoubtedly feeling that merely being identified as one of Schindler's workers meant they had a better chance of staying alive. And they were right.

For one thing, at Emalia there were no daily beatings or indiscriminate killings. "The conditions in Emalia were entirely different than in Plaszow," Irena Schek told a reporter years after the war. "For the first time, we felt safe. We somehow knew that all the things that happened to us could never happen there. And they didn't."[97]

As word spread about this new paradise, people tried to get themselves and their families into Schindler's subcamp, using whatever influence or connections they had to get to Schindler. Occasionally a desperate prisoner would manage to approach Schindler directly, begging him to find a job for an unskilled family member. But Schindler, always wary of a Nazi plot, would sternly send the person away, maintaining that he hired only highly skilled workers.

Within a few days that same family member—someone whom Schindler had never met and had no particular reason to care for or, worse, risk his life for—would suddenly, miraculously be marched under Nazi guard to the safe haven known as Emalia—Schindler's factory. There the Jewish prisoner would be added to the employee list as an experienced metalworker or other highly skilled technician critical to the war effort. "In order to fight the Nazis," one survivor said, "one had to outwit them."[98] And when it came to outsmarting the Nazis, Schindler was a master.

7 The List Is Life: The Liquidation of Plaszow (1944)

By January 1944 the Plaszow forced-labor camp became a *Konzentrationslager*, "concentration camp," under the direct control of officials in Germany. For the Jews this was supposed to mean better living and working conditions since Goeth now reported to the SS office in Berlin, which had informed him that it would not tolerate indiscriminate killings. Yet Malvina Graf says that little changed. "Goeth ignored the new orders," she says, "and used the same drastic measures he always had. We saw no noticeable improvement."[99]

For Schindler the designation of Plaszow as a concentration camp meant that he now had even more officials to pay off in order to get the special favors he wanted and needed. He not only had to keep Amon Goeth happy, he now had to show his gratitude in the form of expensive gifts to high-ranking Nazi officials in Berlin. But Schindler was a master at manipulating

Schindler (second from left) at one of his parties in Kraków. Schindler used parties to bribe Nazi officials and obtain information about imminent deportations.

government officials to get what he wanted. For years he had successfully maneuvered his way around the Nazi bureaucracy through his cunning charm and skillful deceit. As Eva Fogelman puts it, "Drinking with Nazi officials kept him well informed and bribing them with black-market brandy and cigarettes ensured their cooperation."[100] And in the coming months, their cooperation would become essential.

A Health Action

In the spring of 1944 Nazi officials asked Goeth to take an additional seven thousand prisoners into Plaszow. Since the camp was already extremely overcrowded, Goeth explained that the only way he would be able to accommodate the request would be to eliminate many of the prisoners who were already there. He called this elimination process his Health Action, which was held on Sunday, May 7, 1944.

During the Health Action prisoners were forced to strip naked and run back and forth in front of doctors, who would evaluate their physical condition. The doctors would mark down the name of any passing individual whom they found unsuitable. The elderly were an easy target, as were those who appeared physically frail and weak. But even those people who had a slight blemish on their bodies, such as a mole or birthmark, were marked for deportation.

The following week everyone was ordered once again to gather on the *Appelplatz* so that the Nazis could announce who was to be deported. Survivor Malvina Graf relates:

> To the sounds of beautiful classical music, mainly songs for children, such as "Gut Nacht Mutti" (Good Night, Mother) and "Mami, kauf mir ein Pferdchen" (Mama, Buy Me a Pony), which was played for the entire camp through the loudspeakers, 286 children were separated from their mothers.[101]

A Promise to Each Other

Moshe Pantirer describes Amon Goeth in this excerpt taken from the television documentary "Schindler," written by John Blair.

"Goeth took out 50 boys to plant a garden and on the way home, one boy had escaped. Goeth came down with a few SS and he was fuming and yelling, 'Where's the 50th?' We said we didn't know. We couldn't say we saw him escape. So Goeth took every second one of us and was shooting them on the spot. 'That's what happens if anyone of you ever escapes.' So we made a promise that we would be responsible for our friends. How can we save one life and put in jeopardy twenty-five or more?"

A row of ovens reveals the horrifying cremated remains of the bodies of death camp inmates sent to the gas chambers.

In addition, fourteen hundred adults were called out and ordered onto a convoy. The Nazis told the group that they had been selected for *Sonderbehandlung,* "special treatment." Yet by now everyone knew that the Nazis' sadistic term meant only one thing. Soon afterward word came back to the camp that the group had been marched directly into the gas chambers upon arrival at Auschwitz.

A Gift of Hope

During that summer Schindler's actions to help the Jews in his care became even more blatant, even though it meant risking his reputation as an upstanding member of the Nazi Party. It was extremely dangerous for anyone to help Jews in any

way—even for an influential Nazi with important friends in high places. Yet some say that Oskar Schindler thrived on the danger and actually liked taking the enormous risks that put him on the edge of disaster every day.

For example, one day that summer Goeth and Schindler were driving to Goeth's villa when they came upon a group of cattle cars parked along a railroad siding that was waiting for transportation to a death camp in Mauthausen, Austria. From inside the sweltering cattle cars Schindler could hear loud moaning and people begging for water. Stopping the car, Schindler got Goeth's permission to call out the fire department so that he could use their hoses to water down the cars.

Goeth allowed Schindler to do this simply because he found this idea sadistically amusing. In Keneally's words, "If you hosed the cars for people, you were making them promises about a future. And would not such a promise constitute, in anyone's code, a true cruelty?"[102] Therefore, in Goeth's warped mind, this was an excellent idea.

Schindler reportedly also gave some gifts to another officer in exchange for a promise that on the trip to the concentration camp, whenever the train stopped, the officer would open the doors and fill the water cans. One survivor of Mauthausen would always remember these acts of compassion from a man he had never met. "I owe my life to Schindler; without his help I would not have survived the transport nor would I have been strong enough to survive Mauthausen."[103]

A Daring Plan

By the end of the summer of 1944, as the Soviet army advanced westward through Poland, it became apparent to almost everyone that the Germans were losing the war. Consequently the Nazis began to shut down many of their death camps, blow up the crematoriums, and burn the camps' records—all in an effort to destroy evidence of the millions of killings that had taken place in them.

Suddenly word began to spread throughout Plaszow that both the main camp and Schindler's subcamp were to be closed down, and the prisoners, relocated. Everyone knew that relocation meant they were now going to be sent to the death camps.

When Schindler learned of the imminent evacuation of Plaszow, he devised a daring plan to save his workers. Schindler first approached Goeth with his outrageous—perhaps even preposterous—plan at the end of the summer 1944. He had decided, he told Goeth, to build a new factory outside of Poland and to take his workers with him. This new factory would not only serve an essential service to the war effort, but would also serve as a concentration camp as well. He would build this new camp, to the specifications of the SS, at his own expense.

In telling Goeth about his plan, Schindler undoubtedly made it clear how grateful he would be for Goeth's support. With the promise of a nice gratuity, or gift, Goeth promised to support Schindler's plan as long as he could persuade the officials in Berlin to go along with it. Once again, says Wundheiler, Schindler had "to make good use of his acting talent and his talent to persuade and bribe in order to get all the permission slips he needed."[104]

Once his plan was approved, it did not take Schindler long to find a location for his new factory in the small village of Brinnlitz, Czechoslovakia, near Schindler's own hometown of Zwittau. Although there was a great deal of opposition from both the townspeople and certain local party officials to the idea of bringing a bunch of Jews to the town, Schindler overcame objections in his usual manner—a mixture of charm and gratitude in the form of gifts of hard-to-find goods, from vodka to diamonds.

The List

At the same time, Schindler began to put together a list of those factory workers he wanted to take with him to Brinnlitz. In order to convince the Nazis of the importance of these workers, he carefully wrote down next to their names the special skills that made them essential to the war effort.

The rumor spread rapidly throughout Plaszow. "Schindler is going to buy back his workers from the SS," the prisoners said. "There is a list." Suddenly, everyone wanted to be put on the list. "Everyone who could find a way to get on the list did his best [to do so]," recalls Moshe Bejski, a master forger of identification papers in Kraków, who years later became a supreme court judge in Israel.[105]

Schindler put one of his clerks, a man named Marcel Goldberg, in charge of compiling the list. Today most of the survivors have few nice things to say about Goldberg. According to many survivors, Goldberg made it clear that only those Jews who could still afford to pay their way with diamonds or other trade goods would be put on the list. When Pfefferberg heard about the list, for example, he asked his old friend Goldberg to put both him and his wife, Ludmilla, on it. But Goldberg demanded that Pfefferberg give him diamonds first. "You will die here without the diamonds," Pfefferberg remembers Goldberg's saying coldly to him.[106] Eventually Pfefferberg did manage to get both himself and Ludmilla on the list by bribing a sympathetic Nazi officer with a bottle of vodka.

While some people were undoubtedly able to buy their way onto the list, others have no idea how they got on it. Moshe Pantirer says he was put on the list as a metalworker, even though he had never been a metalworker in his life. When asked how he got on the list, he replied, "I would say an angel flew down and put down my name."[107]

Schindler, of course, put some people on the list himself, such as Itzhak Stern, whom Schindler had not only come to rely on and trust, but with whom Schindler had also developed a deep friendship. He also added Helen Rosenzweig, one of Amon Goeth's maids. Years later Rosenzweig told a reporter how she first learned that she was on the list on a day when Schindler came to see her at Goeth's villa:

He said he had a list and was taking all the people on it to his factory in Czechoslovakia. He asked if I had any relatives so I told him about my sisters. I could have put anybody on the list, but nobody was left. My parents, grandmother, cousins, aunts and uncles were gone [dead].[108]

Goeth's Arrest and the Liquidation of Plaszow

On September 13, 1944, to the astonishment of the prisoners at Plaszow, Amon Goeth was arrested by the SS for his black-market activities and for concealing from the Reich a great deal of money and wealth that he had confiscated from the prisoners. He reportedly had been turned in by one of his own subordinates whom Goeth had punished for some minor infraction of one of the camp rules. According to one of the survivors of Plaszow, Goeth was also arrested because a few German civilian officials had heard about the indiscriminate killings in the camp and had objected to them. He was imprisoned in Vienna, Austria.

At the end of September 1944 the long process of liquidating Plaszow began. In order to cover up the evidence of mass murder at Plaszow, a detail of more than one hundred Jews was ordered to dig up the bodies and burn them. In a bitter comment about the gentiles living in the Kraków area who later maintained that

The liquidation of Plaszow meant certain death for those who would be transported to Auschwitz.

they never knew what was going on in Plaszow, Malvina Graf says:

> The brisk autumn winds carried the terrible cloud and the unmistakable odor of burnt flesh far beyond the confines of the camp, well over Krakow and some of the small villages, where lived the people who "never knew what the Nazis were doing" and who "never had any idea that camps even existed."[109]

The Trip Through Gross-Rosen

On Sunday, October 15, 1944, a transport of eight hundred men on Schindler's list left Plaszow in cattle cars, headed for Brinnlitz. Instead of arriving in Brinnlitz, however, they arrived, three days later, at a death camp in Gross-Rosen.

As soon as they arrived, they were ordered to strip and to line up on the *Appelplatz*. "We were kept outside all night for a very exact body search," says Moshe Bejski, "even internal. We were naked all night on a very cold, late October night. I got my clothes at eleven o'clock the next morning."[110]

At Gross-Rosen they were examined by doctors and had numbers tattooed on their arms. Then they waited, not knowing what was to happen next, and no doubt wondering what had happened to their savior, Oskar Schindler.

Finally, three weeks later the eight hundred men were loaded once again onto the freight train, again not knowing for sure where they were headed. "It was always a horrifying thing to go into the trains," says Thomas Keneally. "Even in cold weather, there was a sense of smothering, compounded by blackness."[111] Two days later their train arrived at the station in Zwittau, and from there they were marched to the tiny village of Brinnlitz and to the safety, at last, of Oskar Schindler's factory.

The Women's Trip to Brinnlitz

A week after the men left Plaszow, the three hundred women who were on Schindler's list also left Plaszow for the new camp in Brinnlitz. But their train, too, was diverted, and twelve hours later they arrived at the gates of Auschwitz. As they were ordered out of the freight cars of the train, they were forced to strip and have their heads shaved. They were then sent to the delousing showers. By now everyone had heard the rumors about the showers, and as they entered the showers, the Schindler women must have wondered if at that moment they would be gassed to death.

At about this time Schindler was arrested for the third time—on charges of dealing in the black market. If convicted, he could receive the death penalty. Some say the accusations of black-market activities were initiated by the imprisoned Amon Goeth. Schindler was also accused of bribing Goeth to "go easy on the Jews."

This time it took almost a week for Schindler's connections to effect his release. When he returned to Brinnlitz, he was startled to discover that the women had not arrived but were in Auschwitz, where in all likelihood they would either

Arriving at Brinnlitz

Moshe Bejski told author Eric Silver about the journey from Gross-Rosen to Brinnlitz, in this excerpt from Silver's The Book of the Just: The Unsung Heroes Who Rescued Jews from Hitler.

"The first sign that we were going to Schindler was that they put us in a special barracks. The conditions were so cramped that nobody could sleep for a week. Then one day we were transferred to the wagons, 80–100 in one cattle truck. We went south towards Czechoslovakia. It took another two or three days with only 150 grammes of bread each. We stopped a long time at every station. There were a lot of troop movements. Then we came to Brinnlitz, near Schindler's birthplace, Zwittau. Schindler was not there, the factory equipment had not yet arrived, but we were put in three big rooms on the upper floor. We slept on the floor on loose straw. Later Schindler provided three-tiered bunks with straw in bags. What was important was that we were in Schindler's factory."

soon die from disease and illness or be sent to the gas chambers or be shot. The men at Brinnlitz, whose wives and daughters were among the women at Auschwitz, begged Schindler to do something at once to save them.

Today most people agree that Schindler sent a young woman with gifts of food and liquor and diamonds to negotiate with the SS officials for the release of the women. When she did not return within a few days, Schindler himself went to Auschwitz to settle the matter. Soon afterward the Schindlerfrauen, "Schindler's women," were loaded onto the cattle car for the train trip to Zwittau and the unimaginable safety of Oskar Schindler's safe haven.

8 "I Am the Victim; I Am the Witness": Liberation (1945)

Schindler's factory at Brinnlitz was supposed to be producing munitions parts and artillery shells for the war. But by now Schindler was totally opposed to doing anything that would help the German war effort and continually found ways to make sure that the parts his factory produced did not pass quality control. Later, when certain German officials became suspicious about the lack of quality products coming

out of Schindler's plant, Schindler reportedly bought artillery shells on the black market and passed them off as products of his own factory. Yet he always maintained that his factory in Brinnlitz never produced anything that could be used in the war.

The factory at Brinnlitz, like every other forced-labor camp, was under the watchful eye of the SS. But Schindler made it clear that the guards were neither

The SS, shown here searching Jews for hidden weapons in Warsaw just before the war, were a constant and immediate threat to the safety of Schindler's workers. Even though Schindler bribed and deceived the SS guards assigned to watch over his factory, his workers were in constant danger.

welcome nor permitted on the factory floor or in the dormitories. Consequently he was able to provide much more protection for his workers from SS brutality—something that was unimaginable at Plaszow.

Nevertheless, Schindler was not always able to prevent high-ranking SS officials from coming to the subcamp for inspection. Each time, Schindler greeted them warmly with food and liquor and conviviality, or friendliness, urging them to dine with him first, before making the necessary rounds of the factory. Invariably, by the time the officials got around to going into the factory, they were usually too drunk and in too good a mood to inspect the plant carefully.

The prisoners themselves were also able to use their own skills to deceive the SS officials who came to inspect the plant. As Keneally relates:

> One reason Brinnlitz passed the inspections was the relentless trickery of Oskar's skilled workers. The furnace gauges were rigged by the electricians. The needle registered the correct temperature when the interior of the furnace was in fact hundreds of degrees cooler. . . . [Schindler] would play the somber, baffled manufacturer whose profits were being eroded.[112]

Daily Efforts to Avoid Danger

Despite Schindler's daily efforts to protect his workers, danger was always present. At one inspection, for example, an SS official asked a young man named Jonathan Dresner to start one of the new machines at the plant, but it did not start. Enraged, the officer ordered the young man sent to a concentration camp. Schindler intervened, insisting, as he always did, that the man was a highly skilled munitions worker, essential to the war effort. Nevertheless the SS officer persisted, so Schindler finally suggested that they put the man on trial right then and there. In an elaborate charade, he staged a mock trial. "He put on a real performance," Dresner remembered years later. "Schindler convicted me of breaking the machine and sentenced me to three weeks on the night shift. Then, he came over and kicked and punched me—but not too hard. He had saved my life again."[113]

Schindler also used his influence to remove SS officers who had observed the quality of work a little too closely. Once, an officer reported Schindler to superiors, claiming that Schindler's factory was not really producing anything and that Schindler was merely protecting Jews who had no essential skills at all. As soon as Schindler heard about this complaint, he took action. The officer who had made the claim soon found himself transferred to the front lines.

In another instance high-level officials in Berlin sent word to the head of the SS garrison at Schindler's camp about how to dispose of the Jews in the camp before the Soviets got there. As soon as Schindler heard the orders that the commandant had received, he decided to dispose of the commandant first and, using his influence, had this officer transferred to the front lines, too.

During this time Schindler spent a great deal of time away from the camp, negotiating on the black market for food and other supplies the camp so desperately needed in order to care for the more than one thousand people who lived there. "He rode day and night," Stern later said, "not only to purchase food for the Jews in Brinnlitz camp—but to buy us arms and ammunition in case the SS conceived of killing us during their retreats."[114] He also filled a storehouse at Brinnlitz with tens of thousands of dollars' worth of fabric and textiles for the sole purpose, he later said, "of supplying my Jewish protégés at the end of the war with clothing."[115]

Emilie's Role at Brinnlitz

Emilie joined her husband at Brinnlitz soon after he moved there. It was the first time that the couple had lived together in many years. Apparently Schindler's philandering did not stop just because he and Emilie were once again living together. Ingrid, his longtime mistress, had come to Brinnlitz with Schindler. Moreover, prisoners at Brinnlitz later reported often seeing Schindler in the intimate company of other young women from the village. As Keneally puts it, "The Brinnlitz Oskar was the Oskar old Emalia hands remembered. A bon vivant, a man of wild habits."[116]

During this time Emilie Schindler also took steps to help the prisoners, bringing them food or medicine whenever she could. Once, according to Eric Silver, "she traveled 200 miles to trade two suitcases of vodka—one of the staples of Schindler's black-market commerce—for medicines for them."[117]

Years later Emilie Schindler dismissed her own role in the saving of the Jews. "What I did I did for humanity. I don't need publicity; I don't need songs or whatever. I'm very simple in that sense."[118]

Emilie Schindler, shown in a 1993 photograph, risked her life to help the prisoners, providing them with food and medicine whenever she could.

Other Rescues

During the winter months of 1944–1945 Schindler became even more determined, if not obsessed, in his efforts to rescue as many Jews as possible from the gas chambers of Auschwitz and other death camps. His actions during this time were often impulsive—a word he used years later to describe himself and his rescue attempts. But the word in German means more than just to act spontaneously without careful thought. As Wundheiler points out, the word has "the additional connotation of the presence of an irresistible inner

Schindler, shown here at a 1949 reunion with Itzhak Stern, came to rely on and trust Stern during their years at Kraków and Brinnlitz, and they developed a deep and lasting friendship.

force that drives a person beyond what is considered acceptable behavior."[119]

Fortunately this irresistible inner force compelled Schindler to take action in many different ways. For example, even though he had by now totally abandoned any actual production of munitions, he continued to insist to the SS officials that he needed additional workers in his factory for those essential wartime jobs. In one instance he managed to rescue thirty prisoners from the concentration camp at Gross-Rosen—men he described as skilled metalworkers but who were, in fact, an unknown group of men who had just re-

cently survived a ten-day death march from Auschwitz to Gross-Rosen, during which more than eight thousand other prisoners either died in the subzero temperatures or were killed by the SS.

Schindler also bribed the local police to send him any Jewish escapees rather than turn them over to the SS. In one case two men escaped from a train near the Moravia border on their way to a concentration camp. Later they were captured and put into jail. Schindler was contacted, and soon the men were at Brinnlitz under his care. He reportedly brought eleven more people to the camp in this way.

Another rescue occurred on a freezing January morning in 1945, when a group of about one hundred prisoners from a camp in Golleschau arrived in Zwittau in a cattle car. Today there are two different versions of how this rescue came about. Some say that Schindler was in Kraków at the time and that Emilie was responsible for taking the necessary steps to save the men from almost certain death. In this version of the story, the SS guards reportedly told Emilie that if she didn't take them, they would open the wagon, shoot the prisoners and leave them there. Emilie quickly made the decision to accept the group of men.

In another version of the story Schindler himself heard that there was a freight train in Zwittau with more than one hundred Jews. Supposedly he went to Zwittau and asked a railway official to show him the bill of lading. "When the official was momentarily distracted," says historian Martin Gilbert, Schindler "wrote on it: 'Final destination, Brinnlitz.' Schindler then pointed out to the official that the wagon was intended for his factory."[120]

Schindler immediately called for help to cut open the doors of the freight car, which had been frozen shut. Says Keneally:

It is hard to describe what they saw when the doors were at last opened. In each car, a pyramid of frozen corpses, their limbs madly contorted, occupied the center. The hundred or more still living stank awesomely, were seared black by the cold, were skeletal. Not one of them would be found to weigh more than 75 pounds.[121]

Throughout the war prisoners were packed into the railway cars and deported to unknown destinations, where many met their deaths.

The Horror of the Concentration Camps

The horror of the concentration camps is dramatically captured in this first-person account by an American soldier named Arthur Federman, who helped liberate Poland. This excerpt is from David A. Adler's book We Remember the Holocaust.

"You could smell the camp from at least five miles away. Until then we didn't even know it was ahead. What we saw was horrifying. The Jews were emaciated. You could see their bones. They were all skin and bones. There were bodies piled up in tremendous mounds. Practically all the soldiers became nauseous and threw up."

Prisoners peer from their bunks at Buchenwald concentration camp. Many died from disease, maltreatment, and starvation.

The men were taken to the barracks, where Emilie helped to nurse them back to health. Schindler bought a small piece of property next to a Catholic cemetery in order to establish a Jewish cemetery for the sixteen men who had frozen to death inside the freight car.

By early 1945, some say, Schindler had become totally obsessed with saving as many Jews as possible, regardless of the risks he had to take in order to do so. In an interview for *Entertainment Weekly* magazine Thomas Keneally said:

> A lot of prisoners say that by the end of the war, Oskar was just about out of control. He was traveling around with pockets full of diamonds doing [black market] deals. He was deliberately running along an edge of risk because it suited his temperament.[122]

Liberation

A week before the war ended, Schindler celebrated this thirty-seventh birthday by calling all his factory workers together on the factory floor. He made a speech, pointing out how safe everyone was at his factory. Recalls one survivor:

> He made us stand in silence in memory of our dead people. Somebody might tell you that this was a trick on his part, that this was propaganda for the future to save his skin. I don't know what was going through his mind. What was his motivation I don't know.[123]

Ten days later, on May 7, 1945, Schindler called all of the Jews to the factory floor once again to listen to an impor-

tant radio broadcast. Winston Churchill, prime minister of England, was about to give a speech, announcing the end of the war. "The atmosphere was like [electricity]," remembers Helen Rosenzweig, one of the prisoners who heard Churchill's speech that day, "even though only a few people understood the [English] words."[124]

The broadcast confirmed what everyone had long prayed for but feared would never come: the Germans had surrendered. "Yesterday morning," Churchill solemnly intoned, "at 2:41 A.M. at General Eisenhower's headquarters, [both] the representative of the German High Command and the designated head of the

Schindler in Paris, four years after liberation. At the end of the war Schindler and his wife fled to Switzerland to avoid execution by Soviet troops.

A Final Farewell

A few hours before the end of the war at midnight on May 8, 1945, Schindler called all of the prisoners together for a final farewell speech. This excerpt of that speech is quoted in Thomas Keneally's book Schindler's List.

"The unconditional surrender of Germany has just been announced. After six years of the cruel murder of human beings, victims are being mourned, and Europe is now trying to return to peace and order. I would like to turn to you for unconditional order and discipline—to all of you who together with me have worried through many hard years—in order that you can live through the present and within a few days go back to your destroyed and plundered homes, looking for survivors from your families. . . .

Many of you know the persecutions, the chicanery and obstacles which in order to keep my workers, I had to overcome through many years. If it was already difficult to defend the small rights of the Polish worker, to maintain work for him to prevent him from being sent by force to the Reich, to defend the worker's home and their modest property, then the struggle to defend the Jew workers has often seemed insurmountable. . . .

Don't go into the neighboring houses to rob and plunder. Prove yourselves worthy of the millions of victims among you and refrain from any individual acts of revenge and terror. . . .

Don't thank me for your survival. Thank your people who worked day and night to save you from extermination. Thank your fearless Stern and a few others who, thinking of you and worrying about you, especially in Cracow, have faced death every moment. . . .

In the end, I request you all to keep a three-minute silence, in memory of the countless victims among you who have died in these cruel years."

German State signed the act of unconditional surrender."[125] The war, Churchill said, would end at midnight, May 8.

After the broadcast Schindler spoke solemnly to his workers, most likely calling them "mein kinder" [my children], and telling them that Germany has lost the war. They were saved. According to a transcript of his address that day, he concluded his speech by asking everyone to keep a three-minute silence "in memory of the countless victims among you who have died in these cruel years."[126]

Schindler's Escape

Schindler realized that he and his wife would have to escape immediately. He felt certain that if the Soviets caught him at Brinnlitz, they would execute him on the spot. So Schindler planned to travel toward Switzerland, where he hoped to meet the American forces. Despite the imminent danger, Schindler told his workers once again, "I will not leave you until the last SS man has left the camp." Soon afterward the SS guards quietly departed from Brinnlitz.

Finally it was time for Schindler and Emilie to leave Brinnlitz. As unrealistic as it must have seemed, they attempted to disguise themselves as former prisoners of a labor camp by putting on the striped uniforms of concentration camp inmates. They then set out on their journey to safety in Switzerland, accompanied by eight former prisoners of the Brinnlitz camp as bodyguards.

Before they left, however, the newly liberated prisoners gathered to say goodbye. They gave Schindler a letter to carry with him, attesting to his heroic efforts in saving their lives. Then they gave him one more gift. It was a gold ring, which they had made from the gold dental bridgework of one of the inmates at Brinnlitz. Inside the ring they had inscribed a verse from the Talmud, the body of Jewish law, which poignantly summed up the heroic efforts of Oskar Schindler: "He who saves a single life saves the world entire."[127]

After the War

For the first few years after the war, Oskar and Emilie Schindler lived modestly in Regensburg and Munich, Germany. In 1949 with financial support from a Jewish relief group, Schindler and Emilie, along with Schindler's German mistress, moved to Argentina, taking with them a number of Brinnlitz survivors and their families.

In Argentina Schindler attempted to rebuild his life as an entrepreneur. He started a business raising coypu, small aquatic rodents, for their fur. But within eight years the business had failed, and he went bankrupt. "He was no longer the man he used to be," Emilie told an interviewer years later. "He lost his willpower. He let himself go. He lost the will to fight. He lived hoping something would turn up." His attitude, she says, was "What do I care about tomorrow. Today, I'm here."[128]

In 1958 Schindler left his wife to return to Germany. "Schindler was supposed to come back," Emilie told a reporter matter-of-factly many years later. "But I

Schindler, second from right, surrounded by some of the people he rescued from the death camps of Nazi Germany.

Denying the Holocaust

Today some people deny that the Holocaust ever really occurred. Primo Levi, a survivor of Auschwitz, wrote about the potential consequences of this strange denial, as quoted in Ronnie S. Landau's book The Nazi Holocaust.

"If the world could become convinced that Auschwitz never existed, it would be easier to build a second Auschwitz, and there is no assurance it would devour only Jews."

Civilians give a dignified burial to eight hundred victims of an SS killing.

Schindler at a 1946 reunion in Munich, Germany, with some of the Jews he saved, the Schindlerjuden. When Schindler's businesses failed after the war and he plunged deeply into debt, the survivors of Brinnlitz supported him financially.

think the first thing he did was sell the return ticket. He had mortgaged our farm, so I had to sell it off to pay the bills."[129]

During the next few years in Germany, Schindler tried to start a number of other businesses. They, too, failed, and he never achieved the huge financial success he had achieved in Kraków. During these later years he was both loved and despised—loved by the Jews he had saved and their families, as well as thousands of others who honored his humanitarian efforts, and despised by bigots in Germany who believed that all Jews should have been murdered. At one point he punched a man in the face for calling him a "Jew kisser" and was later sued.

Despite his dire financial situation Schindler never lost his love of a good time and always enjoyed spending money on others. In the 1960s, says Eric Silver, the MGM movie studio gave him an advance of twenty thousand dollars for his life story. Within a week it was gone. That movie was never produced.

An Unhappy Man

In 1963 Pfefferberg contacted all the other survivors of Brinnlitz, asking them to donate at least one day's pay a year to help support Schindler, who, Pfefferberg said at the time, was "discouraged, lonely, and disillusioned."[130] Sol Urbach, a survivor who visited Schindler in Munich twice during those years, agrees, adding that by then Schindler was a very unhappy man and apparently was bordering on paranoia. "He was always looking to see whether someone was following him," says Urbach. "He was unhappy in his marriage. He had come down from such heights, and I think he worried about his past sins."[131]

For the last ten years of his life, Schindler was supported by the Jews he had saved, the Schindlerjuden. Most of the time he lived in Germany. But he would also spend a few months each year in Tel Aviv and Jerusalem, Israel, visiting with many of the survivors and their children.

"He loved children," says Eric Silver. "He saw all the children and grandchildren of those he had rescued as his own family."[132]

In October 1974 in Germany Schindler suddenly, though not unexpectedly, died, his liver ravaged by years of hard drinking. As he had requested, he was buried in Israel in a Catholic cemetery on Mount Zion in Jerusalem. At his funeral many of the Schindlerjuden gathered to pay tribute to the man who had saved their lives. As one observer noted at the time, "[Schindler's] lasting contribution to humanity was vividly etched on those Middle European faces in the pews that day."[133]

On his tombstone in Israel there is a large cross, beneath which are the simple yet poignant words: "The unforgettable life savior of 1,200 oppressed Jews."

Why Did He Do It?

Throughout the years many people have wondered what motivated Oskar Schindler to risk his own life to save a few Jews, when so many other Germans simply turned away. Some skeptics say that he did what he did merely to save his own life. Realizing that the Germans could not win the war, these skeptics say, Schindler put together a cunningly clever plan, designed to save his own neck by saving the lives of a few Jews.

Amon Goeth's mistress, Ruth Kander, knew Schindler during the years of the Plaszow camp. She has maintained that Schindler did what he did for his own sake, that he was merely an opportunist

Relating his story to a reporter in 1963, Schindler displays his collection of photographs taken after the war.

who used the Jews for his own benefit. In a candid interview shortly before her death, she scoffed at the idea that Schindler rescued Jews out of compassion. "Do you think Schindler liked Jews?" she asked the interviewer cynically. "[Do you think] he loved them? Oh, no, no," she insisted, "he needed them, so he worked with them. But he didn't take them into his heart."[134]

There are even a few of the Schindlerjuden who maintain that Schindler actually exploited the Jews by using them as slave labor. They say he used the Jews because they were available and he protected them because he needed them to make money. "After all Schindler was still a German, a Nazi," maintains survivor Joachim Kunstinger. "I'm never going to believe that he was a Jew lover. To me he was a guy who made money."[135]

Another survivor, Jonathan Dresner, believes that Schindler never necessarily intended to save the Jews. It just happened. "He was an adventurer. He was like an actor who always wanted to be centre stage. He got into a play, and he couldn't get out of it."[136]

Even Thomas Keneally says that Schindler hoped that, regardless of who won the war, he would be able to maintain his business and his way of life. "He still hoped, in a way that was almost childlike, that in the new era he would go on being Hans Schindler's successful boy from Zwittau."[137]

His Motives Are Unimportant

On the other hand, most of the Schindlerjuden say that they owe their lives to Oskar Schindler and do not care what his motives were in saving them. He was, in fact, the only German in the history of the war to save more than a thousand Jews. "I don't know what his motives were, even though I knew him very well," says Lewis Fagen. "I asked him and I never got a clear answer. But I don't give a damn. What's important is that he saved our lives."[138] Irena Schek agrees:

Somebody might tell you this was a very smart trick on his part. That this

---

A Question of Motive

In Schindler's List, *Thomas Keneally proffers this explanation of why Schindler chose to undertake a dangerous mission to save the Jews.*

"It can be said to begin with that Oskar was a gambler, was a sentimentalist who loved the transparency, the simplicity of doing good; that Oskar was by temperament an anarchist who loved to ridicule the system; and that beneath the hearty sensuality lay a capacity to be outraged by human savagery, to react to it and to be overwhelmed."

A plaque commemorating Schindler appears in front of a tree planted in Israel in his honor.

was strictly propaganda for the future to save his own skin. I don't know what was going through his mind. This is what happened. What his motivation was, I don't know.[139]

The Reverend Moshe Taube of Pittsburgh also agrees that the question of what Schindler's motivation really was is unimportant. Taube adds, though, that he believes that Schindler was guided in his humanitarian rescue efforts by a higher power. "I believe from the very outset that Schindler was embarking on a humanitarian, divinely inspired mission to save Jews," Taube told Larry King during a television interview in 1994.[140]

Ryszard (Richard) Horowitz, the youngest on Schindler's list, sums up the feelings of most Schindlerjuden when he says: "I feel a certain homage to the man. But whoever [Schindler] was and however he did it, who cares? Life is really what counts."[141]

Schindler's Explanation

Schindler's own explanation for his actions is simple and straightforward. "I knew the people who worked for me," he told Moshe Bejski. "When you know people, you have to behave toward them like human beings."[142]

At another time, recalling those early years in Kraków when Jews were being publicly humiliated and severely persecuted, Schindler said: "There was plenty of public evidence of pure sadism with people behaving like pigs. I felt that the Jews were being destroyed. I had to help them; there was no choice."[143]

Avenue of the Righteous

On August 19, 1953, Israel passed a law called the Martyrs and Heroes Remembrance Act. The purpose of the law was to establish a memorial—Yad Vashem—to those six million Jewish men, women, and children who died during the Holocaust. One part of the law stated that a special place should be set aside to remember those Christians, in particular, who risked their own lives to save the lives of Jewish victims. These men and women are given the title Righteous Ones of the Nations of the World, often simply called Righteous Gentiles. For each person who is recognized as a Righteous Gentile, there is a special ceremony during which a carob

One of the Righteous

Author Eric Silver writes about Oskar Schindler's complex personality in The Book of the Just: The Unsung Heroes Who Rescued Jews from Hitler.

"You had to take him as he was. Schindler was a very complex person. Schindler was a good human being. He was against evil. He acted spontaneously. He was adventurous, someone who took risks, but I'm not sure he enjoyed taking them. He did things because people asked him to do them. He loved children. He saw all the children and grandchildren of those he had rescued as his own family. He was very, very sensitive. If Schindler had been a normal man, he would not have done what he did. Everything he did put him in danger. He could have done much less, and still qualified as one of the righteous."

Schindler, named a Righteous Gentile in 1963, stands next to the carob tree that commemorates his heroic rescue actions.

tree is planted along the Avenue of the Righteous Among the Nations, which leads to the Yad Vashem Holocaust Memorial.

For a person to be named a Righteous Gentile, it has to be shown that that person took an active role in helping to save Jews from destruction during the Holocaust. It is not enough for "a Christian to express sympathy for Jews or even to pray for them in their terminal misery. Action had to be the order of the day, however inconvenient or dangerous."[144] Clearly, there were many good people who did not support the Nazi policies. But as Zev Kadem, one of the Schindlerjuden points out: "It's not enough to be good. One has to act against evil."[145]

A Righteous Gentile

In 1963 Oskar Schindler was named a Righteous Gentile. He was the third Christian to receive this honor. According to Moshe Bejski, who has served for many years on the committee that decided who will be honored as a Righteous Gentile, "Schindler was unique in two ways: he carried on his rescue actions for a very long time, and he did it on a large scale."[142] Included with this honor was a medal inscribed with the words "In gratitude from the Jewish people."

Years after the war there were still those who maintained that there was nothing they could have done to prevent the slaughter of so many millions of human beings. As Amon Goeth's former mistress asked a reporter during an interview late in her life, "What could we have done?" Pausing to reflect for a moment, she then answered her own question. "Nothing," she insisted. "We couldn't do anything against it."[147]

Oskar Schindler proved she was wrong. He showed that there were many things one could do to stand up against the ugly depravity, hatred, and injustice that existed at that time.

The importance of Oskar Schindler to the lives of more than eleven hundred people, then, is obvious. Without his humanitarian efforts many of these people—perhaps all of them—would have died of illness or starvation or would have been viciously murdered in the gas chambers of Poland.

But Oskar Schindler is important for another reason. The atrocities that occurred during the twelve years that Hitler ruled the German empire are, in the words of Tadeusz Pankiewicz, "irrefutable proof of the depths to which blind hatred and insensitivity can sink."[148] Yet the actions of Oskar Schindler and hundreds of other individuals like him are equally irrefutable proof that one person can stand up against bigotry, prejudice, and intolerance and, in doing so, make a difference. His example is a testament to the importance of Oskar Schindler.

Afterword

- On April 30, 1945, one week before the end of World War II, Adolf Hitler committed suicide.

- On September 13, 1946, an unrepentant and unremorseful Amon Goeth was hanged in Kraków for his war crimes.

- Hans Frank was tried among the major Nazi war criminals and hanged at Nuremberg.

- In 1956, Abraham Bankier died of a heart attack in Vienna.

- In 1969 Itzhak Stern died in Tel Aviv. Schindler was devastated and reportedly cried uncontrollably.

- On October 25, 1980, author Thomas Keneally went into a Beverly Hills, California, leather goods shop to buy a briefcase. He met the owner of the shop, who, upon learning that Keneally was a writer, began to tell him the amazing story of Oskar Schindler. Two years later Keneally published the story under the title *Schindler's Ark*, later titled *Schindler's List*.

- In 1993 director Steven Spielberg produced and directed an Academy Award-winning movie based on the book. At the awards ceremony Spielberg thanked the man who had first brought the story to Keneally's attention—a man who had lived through the hell called the Holocaust—Leopold Page, Leopold Pfefferberg.

- In 1995, Emilie Schindler, now in her eighties, lives alone in Argentina.

- Today only a handful of Jews still live in Kraków, Poland.

Notes

Introduction: An Unlikely Savior

1. Elizabeth Gleick, "Requiem for a Hero," *People Weekly*, March 21, 1994, p. 43.

2. John Blair, "Schindler." Television documentary. London: Thames T.V., 1983.

3. Blair, "Schindler."

4. Luitgard N. Wundheiler, "Oskar Schindler's Moral Development During the Holocaust," *Humbolt Journal of Social Relations*, Fall/Winter–Spring/Summer, 1985–1986, p. 334.

5. The Reverend Moshe Taube, on *Larry King Live*, transcript #1046. Air date: February 17, 1994.

6. Wundheiler, "Oskar Schindler's Moral Development During the Holocaust," p. 336.

7. Martin Gilbert, *The Holocaust: A History of the Jews of Europe During the Second World War.* New York: Henry Holt and Company, 1985, p. 824.

8. Ronnie S. Landau, *The Nazi Holocaust.* Chicago: Ivan R. Dee, 1992, p. 216.

9. Wundheiler, "Oskar Schindler's Moral Development During the Holocaust," p. 337.

10. Don Podesta, "A Widow's Memories of a Flawed Saint," *The Washington Post,* December 15, 1993, p. B1

11. H. D. Leuner, *When Compassion Was a Crime.* London: Oswald Wolff, 1966, p. 94

12. Gay Block and Malka Drucker, *Rescuers: Portraits of Moral Courage in the Holocaust.* New York: Holmes & Meier Publishers, 1992, p. 10

13. Sholem Asch, quoted in Philip Friedman, *Their Brothers' Keepers.* New York: Crown Publishers, 1957, p. 13.

Chapter 1: An Uneventful Youth (1908–1938)

14. Milton Meltzer, *Never to Forget: The Jews of the Holocaust.* New York: Harper & Row, 1976, p. 192.

15. Thomas Keneally, *Schindler's List.* New York: Simon & Schuster, 1982, p. 33.

16. Bernard Scheuer, quoted in *The Christian Century*, February 16, 1994, p. 164.

17. Keneally, *Schindler's List*, p. 37.

18. Emilie Schindler, quoted in Blair, "Schindler."

19. Wundheiler, "Oskar Schindler's Moral Development During the Holocaust," p. 335.

20. Wundheiler, "Oskar Schindler's Moral Development During the Holocaust," p. 335.

21. Landau, *The Nazi Holocaust*, p. 135.

22. Keneally, *Schindler's List*, p. 37.

23. Keneally, *Schindler's List*, p. 40.

24. Landau, *The Nazi Holocaust*, p. 147.

Chapter 2: The Rise of Adolf Hitler

25. Adolf Hitler, as quoted in *Scholastic Update*, April 2, 1993, p. 6.

26. Landau, *The Nazi Holocaust*, p. 94.

27. Meltzer, *Never to Forget*, p. 11.

28. Leuner, *When Compassion Was a Crime*, p. 19.

29. Point 4 of "The Nazi Party's 25-Point Programme of 1920," quoted in Landau, *The Nazi Holocaust*, p. 122.

30. Adolf Hitler, quoted in Leuner, *When Compassion Was a Crime*, p. 17.

31. Gilbert, *The Holocaust*, p. 53.

32. Adolf Hitler, quoted in Block and Drucker, *Rescuers*, p. 133.

33. Azriel Eisenberg, *Witness to the Holocaust*. New York: Pilgrim Press, 1981, p. 35.

34. Martin Luther, *On the Jews and Their Lives* (Wittenberg, 1543), quoted in Block and Drucker, *Rescuers*, p. 132.

35. Wilhelm Marr, quoted in Meltzer, *Never to Forget*, p. 8.

36. David A. Adler, *We Remember the Holocaust*. New York: Henry Holt and Company, 1989, p. 6.

37. Leo Baeck, quoted in Eric Boehm, *We Survived: Fourteen Histories of the Hidden and Hunted of Nazi Germany*. Santa Barbara, CA: Clio Press, 1966, p. 284.

38. Heinrich Heine, quoted in Landau, *The Nazi Holocaust*, p. 126.

39. Cheryl Crabtree, *Beit Hashoah—Museum of Tolerance*. Los Angeles: Simon Wiesenthal Center, 1993, p. 31.

40. Block and Drucker, *Rescuers*, p. 159.

Chapter 3: Arrival in Kraków (1939–1940)

41. Gilbert, *The Holocaust*, p. 87.

42. Block and Drucker, *Rescuers*, p. 159.

43. Malvina Graf, *The Krakow Ghetto and the Plaszow Camp Remembered*. Tallahassee: Florida State University Press, 1989, p. 7.

44. Meltzer, *Never to Forget*, p. 59.

45. Meltzer, *Never to Forget*, p. 78.

46. Gilbert, *The Holocaust*, p. 101.

47. Emmanuel Ringelblum, *Notes from the Warsaw Ghetto: The Journal of Emmanuel Ringelblum*. New York: Schocken Books, 1958, p. 37.

48. Wundheiler, "Oskar Schindler's Moral Development During the Holocaust," p. 343.

49. Hans Frank, quoted in Gilbert, *The Holocaust*, p. 106.

50. Eva Fogelman, *Conscience and Courage: Rescuers of Jews During the Holocaust*. New York: Doubleday, 1994, p. 181.

51. Emilie Schindler, quoted in Blair, "Schindler."

52. Keneally, *Schindler's List*, p. 83.

53. Keneally, *Schindler's List*, p. 70.

54. Keneally, *Schindler's List*, p. 74.

55. Léon Poliakov, *Harvest of Hate: The Nazi Program for the Destruction of the Jews of Europe*. New York: Holocaust Library, 1979, p. 84.

Chapter 4: The Establishment of the Kraków Ghetto (1941)

56. Landau, *The Nazi Holocaust*, p. 155.

57. Keneally, *Schindler's List*, p. 87.

58. Graf, *The Krakow Ghetto*, p. 9.

59. Meltzer, *Never to Forget*, p. 78.

60. Tadeusz Pankiewicz, *The Cracow Ghetto Pharmacy*. Translated by Henry Tilles. New York: Holocaust Library, 1947, p. 3.

61. Graf, *The Krakow Ghetto*, p. 40.

62. Graf, *The Krakow Ghetto*, p. 40.

63. Graf, *The Krakow Ghetto*, p. 38.

64. Wundheiler, "Oskar Schindler's Moral Development During the Holocaust," p. 337.

65. Eric Silver, *The Book of the Just: The Unsung Heroes Who Rescued Jews from Hitler*. New York: Grove Press, 1992, p. 149.

66. Ester Kaufman, quoted in Katherine Monk, "Fate and Schindler: Vancouver Residents Ester Kaufman and Bernard Goldman Say There Are Only Two Reasons They Survived the Holocaust," *Vancouver Sun*, January 25, 1994, C5.

67. Wundheiler, "Oskar Schindler's Moral Development During the Holocaust," p. 345.

68. Landau, *The Nazi Holocaust*, p. 175.

69. Gilbert, *The Holocaust*, p. 246.

Chapter 5: No Exceptions; No Mercy: The Turning Point (1942)

70. Keneally, *Schindler's List*, p. 123.

71. Graf, *The Krakow Ghetto*, p. 43.

72. Pankiewicz, *The Cracow Ghetto Pharmacy*, p. 45.

73. Keneally, *Schindler's List*, p. 130.

74. Oskar Schindler, quoted in Keneally, *Schindler's List*, p. 133.

75. Pankiewicz, *The Cracow Ghetto Pharmacy*, p. 59.

76. Keneally, *Schindler's List*, p. 136.

77. Pankiewicz, *The Cracow Ghetto Pharmacy*, p. 60.

78. Keneally, *Schindler's List*, p. 155.

79. Wundheiler, "Oskar Schindler's Moral Development During the Holocaust," p. 338.

Chapter 6: "An Hour of Life Is Still Life": Establishing a Camp at Plaszow (1943)

80. Graf, *The Krakow Ghetto*, p. 93.

81. Sol Urbach, quoted in Blair, "Schindler."

82. Pankiewicz, *The Cracow Ghetto Pharmacy*, p. 115.

83. Moshe Pantirer, quoted in Blair, "Schindler."

84. Graf, *The Krakow Ghetto*, p. 77.

85. Sol Urbach, quoted in Jacquie Asplundh, "Schindler's List Survivor Brings Message to WW-P," *Princeton Packet*, March 11, 1994, p. 1.

86. Sol Urbach, quoted in Asplundh, "Schindler's List Survivor Brings Message to WW-P," p. 11A.

87. Shmuel Krakowski, *The War of the Doomed: Jewish Resistance in Poland, 1942–1944*. New York: Holmes & Meier Publishers, 1984, p. 236.

88. Henry Wermeuth, quoted in Anton Gill, *The Journey Back from Hell: Conversations with Concentration Camp Survivors: An Oral History*. New York: Avon Books, 1988, p. 197.

89. Graf, *The Krakow Ghetto*, p. 106.

90. Keneally, *Schindler's List*, p. 164.

91. Pankiewicz, *The Cracow Ghetto Pharmacy*, p. 111.

92. Gleick, "Requiem for a Hero," p. 45.

93. Helen Rosenzweig, quoted in Annette

Wexler, "A Real Life Story of Schindler's List," *New York Times*, February 27, 1994, sec: 13NJ, p.1.

94. Helen Rosenzweig, quoted in Wexler, "A Real Life Story of Schindler's List," sec: 13NJ, p.1.

95. Keneally, *Schindler's List*, p. 170.

96. Keneally, *Schindler's List*, p. 194.

97. Irena Schek, quoted in Blair, "Schindler."

98. Wundheiler, "Oskar Schindler's Moral Development During the Holocaust," p. 351.

Chapter 7: The List Is Life: The Liquidation of Plaszow (1944)

99. Graf, *The Krakow Ghetto*, p. 112.

100. Fogelman, *Conscience and Courage*, p. 9.

101. Graf, *The Krakow Ghetto*, p. 124.

102. Keneally, *Schindler's List*, p. 266.

103. Wundheiler, "Oskar Schindler's Moral Development During the Holocaust," p. 353.

104. Wundheiler, "Oskar Schindler's Moral Development During the Holocaust," p. 349.

105. Silver, *The Book of the Just*, p. 150.

106. Leopold Pfefferberg, quoted in Blair, "Schindler."

107. Murray Pantirer, quoted in Blair, "Schindler."

108. Helen Rosenzweig, quoted in Wexler, "A Real Life Story of Schindler's List," sec: 13NJ, p.1.

109. Graf, *The Krakow Ghetto*, p. 133.

110. Silver, *The Book of the Just*, p. 151.

111. Keneally, *Schindler's List*, p. 326.

Chapter 8: "I Am the Victim; I Am the Witness": Liberation (1945)

112. Keneally, *Schindler's List*, p. 343.

113. Eric Silver, "A Crook, a Womanizer, and a Hero," *MacLean's*, January 17, 1994, p. 52.

114. Itzhak Stern, quoted in Keneally, *Schindler's List*, p. 337.

115. Keneally, *Schindler's List*, p. 374.

116. Keneally, *Schindler's List*, p. 335.

117. Silver, *The Book of the Just*, p. 152.

118. Podesta, "A Widow's Memories of a Flawed Saint," p. B1.

119. Wundheiler, "Oskar Schindler's Moral Development During the Holocaust," p. 340.

120. Gilbert, *The Holocaust*, p. 777.

121. Keneally, *Schindler's List*, p. 355.

122. Thomas Keneally, quoted in Steve Daly, "Some Kind of Hero," *Entertainment Weekly*, December 12, 1993, p. 45.

123. Blair, "Schindler."

124. Helen Rosenzweig, quoted in Wexler, "A Real Life Story of Schindler's List," sec: 13NJ, p. 1.

125. Winston Churchill, quoted in Blair, "Schindler."

126. Keneally, *Schindler's List*, p. 372.

127. Keneally, *Schindler's List*.

Epilogue: After the War

128. Emilie Schindler, quoted on Blair, "Schindler."

129. Emilie Schindler, quoted in Michael Neill, "An Angel Looks Homeward," *People Weekly*, December 13, 1993, p. 58.

130. Leopold (Poldek) Pfefferberg, quoted in Keneally, *Schindler's List*, p. 395.

131. Sol Urbach, quoted in Asplundh, "Schindler's List Survivor Brings Message to WW-P," p. 11A.

132. Silver, "A Crook, a Womanizer, and a Hero," p. 52.

133. Blair, "Schindler."

134. Ruth Kander, quoted in Blair, "Schindler."

135. Joachim Kunstinger, quoted in Blair, "Schindler."

136. Jonathan Dresner, quoted in Silver, "A Crook, a Womanizer, and a Hero," p. 52.

137. Keneally, *Schindler's List*, p. 137.

138. Lewis Fagen, quoted in David Margolick, "Schindler's Jews Find Deliverance Again," *New York Times*, February 13, 1994, sec: 4, p. 1.

139. Irena Schek, quoted in Blair, "Schindler."

140. The Reverend Moshe Taube, on *Larry King Live*.

141. Richard Horowitz, quoted in Blair, "Schindler."

142. Silver, *The Book of the Just*, p. 148.

143. Oskar Schindler, quoted in Blair, "Schindler."

144. Peter Hellman, *Avenue of the Righteous: Portraits in Uncommon Courage of Christians and the Jews They Saved from Hitler*. New York: Atheneum, 1980, p. vii.

145. Zev Kadem, quoted in Gleick, "Requiem for a Hero," p. 45.

146. Moshe Bejski, quoted in Wundheiler, "Oskar Schindler's Moral Development During the Holocaust," p. 334.

147. Ruth Kander, quoted in Blair, "Schindler."

148. Pankiewicz, *The Cracow Ghetto Pharmacy*, p. 123.

For Further Reading

David A. Adler, *We Remember the Holocaust.* New York: Henry Holt and Company, 1989. Good introduction to the Holocaust for upper elementary and middle school students, including many personal testimonies and remembrances.

Linda Atkinson, *In Kindling Flame: The Story of Hannah Senesh,* 1921–1944. New York: William Morrow, 1992. Excellent biography for middle school students of a heroic young Jewish-Hungarian resistance fighter.

Anne Frank, *The Diary of a Young Girl.* New York: Pocket Books, 1953. The classic personal account of a young Jewish girl and her family in hiding during the Holocaust.

Howard Greenfield, *The Hidden Children.* New York: Trickman and Fields, 1993. Describes the experiences of children forced into hiding during the Holocaust.

Andrew Handler and Susan V. Meschel, eds., *Young People Speak: Surviving the Holocaust in Hungary.* New York: Franklin Watts, 1993. Eleven survivors tell about their childhood during the Holocaust.

Elaine Landau, *Warsaw Ghetto Uprising.* New York: Macmillan, 1992. An excellent, in-depth account of the Warsaw ghetto, focusing primarily on the twenty-eight days of the Warsaw ghetto uprising.

Milton Meltzer, *Never to Forget: The Jews of the Holocaust.* New York: Harper & Row, 1976. Excellent book for junior high school students. Focuses on the Holocaust, the history of anti-Semitism, and Jewish resistance.

———, *Rescue: The Story of How Gentiles Saved Jews in the Holocaust.* New York: Harper & Row, 1988. Popular author for young people focuses on the stories of non-Jews who risked their lives to save Jews during the Holocaust.

Hans Richter, *Friedrich.* New York: Puffin Books, 1987. An easy-to-read autobiographical novel of two German boys, one Jewish and one not, during the Holocaust.

Elie Wiesel, *Night.* New York: Bantam, 1982. Beautifully written memoir of the author's experience at Auschwitz.

Additional Works Consulted

Wladyslaw Bartoszewski and Zofia Lewin, *The Samaritans: Heroes of the Holocaust.* New York: Twayne Publishers Inc., 1970. Stories of the courageous men and women who risked their own lives to save victims from the Holocaust.

Gay Block and Malka Drucker, *Rescuers: Portraits of Moral Courage in the Holocaust.* New York: Holmes & Meier Publishers, 1992. Interviews with forty-nine individuals from ten countries who risked their lives to save others during the Holocaust.

Eric Boehm, *We Survived: Fourteen Histories of the Hidden and Hunted of Nazi Germany.* Santa Barbara, CA: Clio Press, 1966. Personal testimonies of fourteen Jews who hid during the Holocaust.

Elinor J. Brecher, *Schindler's Legacy.* New York: Penguin Books, 1994. Dramatic and moving in-depth biographies of more than thirty Schindlerjuden, including accounts of their present-day lives.

Azriel Eisenberg, *Witness to the Holocaust.* New York: Pilgrim Press, 1981. An excellent anthology of the Holocaust from the beginning of the Third Reich through liberation.

Gerald Fleming, *Hitler and the Final Solution.* Berkeley: The University of California Press, 1984. Based on thorough research, this book proves that Hitler personally and deliberately planned the annihilation of all European Jews.

Eva Fogelman, *Conscience and Courage: Rescuers of Jews During the Holocaust.* New York: Doubleday, 1994. A psychologist's look at the characteristics of those men and women who risked their lives to save Jews during the Holocaust.

Philip Friedman, *Their Brothers' Keepers.* New York: Crown Publishers, 1957. A look at the rescue activities of Christians during the Holocaust.

Martin Gilbert, *The Holocaust: A History of the Jews of Europe During the Second World War.* New York: Henry Holt and Company, 1985. Thorough, well-documented history of the Holocaust.

Anton Gill, *The Journey Back from Hell: Conversations with Concentration Camp Survivors: An Oral History.* New York: Avon Books, 1988. Focuses on survivors' lives after liberation.

Malvina Graf, *The Krakow Ghetto and the Plaszow Camp Remembered.* Tallahassee: Florida State University Press, 1989. Engrossing first-person account of life in the Kraków ghetto and the Plaszow concentration camp.

Peter Hellman, *Avenue of the Righteous: Portraits in Uncommon Courage of Christians and the Jews They Saved from Hitler.* New York: Atheneum, 1980. The story of four of the Righteous Gentiles and those they saved during the war.

Thomas Keneally, *Schindler's List.* New York: Simon & Schuster, 1982. A gripping, fact-based novel; the definitive story of the life of Oskar Schindler.

Shmuel Krakowski, *The War of the Doomed: Jewish Resistance in Poland, 1942–1944.* New York: Holmes & Meier Publishers, 1984. Describes the history and basic aspects of the Jewish resistance in Poland during the Holocaust.

Ronnie S. Landau, *The Nazi Holocaust.* Chicago: Ivan R. Dee, 1992. Though difficult reading, an excellent history of the Holocaust and its moral, ethical, and psychological implications. Includes an extensive bibliography.

H. D. Leuner, *When Compassion Was a Crime.* London: Oswald Wolff, 1966. Tells the story of men and women who put their own lives in jeopardy to rescue Hitler's victims.

Tadeusz Pankiewicz, *The Cracow Ghetto Pharmacy.* Translated by Henry Tilles. New York: Holocaust Library, 1947. Excellent eyewitness account of daily life in the Kraków ghetto by a non-Jewish Pole.

Léon Poliakov, *Harvest of Hate: The Nazi Program for the Destruction of the Jews of Europe.* New York: Holocaust Library, 1979. First published in 1954, this is an early study of the Nazis' plan for the Final Solution.

Emmanuel Ringelblum, *Notes from the Warsaw Ghetto: The Journal of Emmanuel Ringelblum.* New York: Schocken Books, 1958. Famous diary of a historian imprisoned in the Warsaw ghetto.

Seymour Rossel, *The Holocaust.* New York: Franklin Watts, 1981. A historical account of the Holocaust, including how it was organized and carried out; also discusses its aftermath.

Eric Silver, *The Book of the Just: The Unsung Heroes Who Rescued Jews from Hitler.* New York: Grove Press, 1992. Tells the stories of forty heroes of the Holocaust, including Oskar Schindler.

Luitgard N. Wundheiler, "Oskar Schindler's Moral Development During the Holocaust," *Humboldt Journal of Social Relations*, Fall/Winter–Spring/Summer, 1985–1986.

Magazine Articles

Jonathan Alter, "After the Survivors," *Newsweek*, December 20, 1993.

David Ansen, "Spielberg's Obsession," *Newsweek*, December 20, 1993.

Herbert Buchsbaum, "Anatomy of the Holocaust," *Scholastic Update*, April 2, 1993.

The Christian Century, "Firsthand Testimony to Oskar Schindler," February 16, 1994.

Steve Daly, "Some Kind of Hero," *Entertainment Weekly*, December 12, 1993.

Catherine Foster, "Australian Writer Tells the Story Behind the Story," *Christian Science Monitor*, December 15, 1993.

Owen Gleiberman, "Dark Victory," *Entertainment Weekly*, December 17, 1993.

Elizabeth Gleick, "Requiem for a Hero," *People Weekly*, March 21, 1994.

Michael Neill, "An Angel Looks Homeward," *People Weekly*, December 13, 1993.

Eric Silver, "A Crook, a Womanizer, and a Hero," *MacLean's*, January 17, 1994.

Time, "Heart of Darkness," December 13, 1993.

Newspaper Articles

Jacquie Asplundh, "Schindler's List Survivor Brings Message to WW-P," *Princeton Packet*, March 11, 1994.

Richard Cohen, "Schindler's Lesson," *Washington Post*, December 14, 1993.

David Margolick, "Schindler's Jews Find Deliverance Again," *New York Times*, February 13, 1994.

Katherine Monk, "Fate and Schindler: Vancouver Residents Ester Kaufman and Bernard Goldman Say There Are Only Two Reasons They Survived the Holocaust," *Vancouver Sun*, January 25, 1994.

Don Podesta, "A Widow's Memories of a Flawed Saint," *Washington Post*, December 15, 1993.

Annette Wexler, "A Real Life Story of Schindler's List," *New York Times*, February 27, 1994.

Television Productions

John Blair, "Schindler," Television documentary. London: Thames T.V., 1983.

Larry King Live, transcript #1046. Air date: February 17, 1994. Schindler survivors and an actor, Liam Neeson, portraying Schindler.

The Oprah Winfrey Show, "Real-Life Schindler's List," March 18, 1994.

The Phil Donahue Show, transcript #3935. National feed date: February 28, 1994.

Index

Picture Credits

Cover photo: Herbert Steinhouse, courtesy of the United States Holocaust Memorial Museum/Al Taylor

AP/Wide World Photos, 35, 91

Archives of the State Museum, Oswiecim/ Courtesy of the Simon Wiesenthal Center Beit HaShoah Museum of Tolerance Library/Archives, Los Angeles, CA, 9

Lisa Berg, United States Holocaust Memorial Museum, 79

Bildarchiv Preussischer Kulterbesitz/ Courtesy of the Simon Wiesenthal Center Beit HaShoah Museum of Tolerance Library/Archives, Los Angeles, CA, 30, 77

Bundesarchiv/Courtesy of the Simon Wiesenthal Center Beit HaShoah Museum of Tolerance Library/ Archives, Los Angeles, CA, 61

Bundesarchiv Koblenz/Courtesy of the Simon Wiesenthal Center Beit HaShoah Museum of Tolerance Library/Archives, Los Angeles, CA, 32, 44

Dachau Concentration Camp Memorial/ Courtesy of the Simon Wiesenthal Center Beit HaShoah Museum of Tolerance Library/Archives, Los Angeles, CA, 57 (bottom)

Der Stuermer, January 1934/Courtesy of the Simon Wiesenthal Center Beit HaShoah Museum of Tolerance Library/Archives, Los Angeles, CA, 21

Ein Bilderbuch fuer Gross und Klein, Nuremberg, 1936/Courtesy of the Simon Wiesenthal Center Beit HaShoah Museum of Tolerance Library/ Archives, Los Angeles, CA, 31

Avi Granot, courtesy of the United States Holocaust Memorial Museum, 88

Leo Baeck Institute, NY/Courtesy of the Simon Wiesenthal Center Beit HaShoah Museum of Tolerance Library/Archives, Los Angeles, CA, 45

Library of Congress, 18, 26, 33

Main Commission for the Investigation of Nazi War Crimes, Warsaw, Poland, courtesy of the United States Holocaust Memorial Museum, 74

National Archives, 13, 24, 25, 29, 55, 57 (top), 71, 81, 82, 87

Professor Leopold Pfefferberg-Page, courtesy of the United States Holocaust Memorial Museum, 11, 19, 39, 49, 53, 59, 62, 63, 64, 66, 69, 86, 92

Courtesy of the Simon Wiesenthal Center Beit HaShoah Museum of Tolerance Library/Archives, Los Angeles, CA, 36, 41, 43, 51

Stadarchiva Bielefeld/Courtesy of the Simon Wiesenthal Center Beit HaShoah Museum of Tolerance Library/Archives, Los Angeles, CA, 47

Herbert Steinhouse, courtesy of the United States Holocaust Memorial Museum, 15

Herbert Steinhouse, courtesy of the United States Holocaust Memorial Museum/Al Taylor, 80, 83

UPI/Bettmann, 16, 89

Yad Vashem Archives, 37, 48

Yad Vashem, Jerusalem, Israel, courtesy of the United States Holocaust Memorial Museum, 67

About the Author

For more than twenty-five years, Jack L. Roberts has worked as an editor and writer of educational materials for elementary and junior high school students and teachers, first at Children's Television Workshop and then at Scholastic Inc.

In addition, he has written several books for young readers, including a junior high school textbook on computer literacy as well as biographies of President Bill Clinton, South African civil rights leader Nelson Mandela, and U.S. Supreme Court Justice Ruth Bader Ginsburg.